WINNING STRATEGIES FOR SPORTS AND LIFE

To Stewart,

Wishing you all the best
and hope This helps you
become even more of a
winner!

Midge xxx

GW00578164

WINNING STRATEGIES FOR SPORTS AND LIFE

Midgie Thompson

First Published in Great Britain 2013 by
Gabrielle Lea Publishing, London

© Copyright Midgie Thompson 2013

Cover design by Natalie Wunn

Edited by Christina Harkness

ISBN: 978-0-9572186-2-8

To all those who have joined me on this journey.

Acknowledgements

I would particularly like to thank Gabby for her continued friendship, support and encouragement.

I would like to thank Lloyd who got me started on this running journey.

I would also like to thank all the clients who worked with me and helped me learn so much. I am very grateful to have had you, and still have you, in my life.

Additional thanks goes to Christina for stepping in at the end and providing invaluable support and expertise, to Roger and Emily who helped get me started on my NLP journey and the University of Brighton for their flexibility, which enabled me to complete this book.

Contents

Preface   i

Introduction   1

Getting Started   3
    Goals and Motivation   5
    Values and Beliefs   25
    Self Management   41
    Life Balance   59

Mental Preparation   71
    Confidence   73
    Internal Dialogue   91
    Mental Rehearsal   103

Event Performance   113
    Relaxation   115
    Routines   129
    Focus   143

Post Event Review   161
    Review, Reflect and Plan   163

Conclusion   175

Winning Strategies Summary   179

About Midgie   181
    Contacting the author   182

References   183

Bibliography   185

Preface

I thought I would give you a bit of background to how this Winning Strategies process came about. This is a very personal story because I actually lived the steps described in this book to help me as I recovered from an illness and ran my first marathon eleven months later. I wasn't even a long distance runner before then! Now, after years of using these steps with sports and business clients to help them achieve peak levels of performance, I am finally sharing them with you.

In 1999, I became quite ill with something like glandular fever that caused me to be bedridden and unable to eat. Now, the fact that I was holding down two jobs and burning the proverbial candle at both ends and in the middle, it was not really that surprising that I became ill. My body decided it did not want to play that game anymore! The lifestyle I was leading was neither healthy nor sustainable on so many levels.

As my health steadily improved and I started to regain my strength, I went from a time of struggling to simply walk down the street because I was so weak to being able to run a 10K race. A very good friend, Lloyd, challenged me to try running in a local 10K race. Lloyd encouraged me, cajoled me and teased me into accepting the challenge to have the goal of simply 'crossing the finish line' regardless of how long it took. The gauntlet of running the race was thrown down and, of course, I had to pick it up. Even though I didn't really believe I could actually do the distance, I agreed to have a go as I always enjoyed challenges.

Well, I did it! I ran my first 10K race, just five months after I had been ill! I thought to myself, "If I can do this, what else can I do? What other goals can I set myself and achieve?"

After finishing that race, I was not happy with simply rejoining the human race, being a productive member of society and holding down a full-time job again; I decided to train and prepare to run a marathon. I chose to return to my hometown of Ottawa, Canada in May 2000 to run my very first marathon race.

I effectively lived all the principles I describe in this book. I needed an excuse to help me live a healthier lifestyle and take better care of my health. The goal of running a marathon was certainly a strong incentive to lead a healthier lifestyle! I had no choice! I had to lead a healthy lifestyle so I could work as well as do the required marathon training.

I overcame doubts and fears I had about accomplishing my goals, and I learned to believe in myself and believe that anything is possible if I put my mind to it. With help, support and encouragement from my fellow running mates, I gradually built my confidence.

Even though my confidence grew during training, when a smaller race day arrived, I was a nervous wreck because I was afraid I'd forget something; I was afraid I couldn't do it, and I was afraid that I wouldn't be good enough. All this nervousness was draining me of my energy, made me feel weak and tired, even before I started to run! I knew I had to develop strategies to calm those race nerves, focus on what was essential for me to run and have a pre-event routine that was calmingly familiar.

When I actually got to that marathon, eleven months after I had been bedridden and ill, I had a personal mantra which was 'I CAN and I AM'. I wanted to prove to myself, and to everyone who doubted me, that I could actually do it! And, I did!

Afterwards, as I contemplated all that I had done to get me to running my first marathon, I realized that the same approach could be used in many others areas in life where people want to switch themselves on and be the best they can be for a particular performance event such as a race. I started using these strategies with clients and saw great results.

This peak performance process is now contained in this book. Here are the *Winning Strategies* that will help you be the best you can be in your sport and your life!

Midgie Thompson
March 2013

PREFACE

Introduction

Success in sport comes from more than simply doing all the necessary physical training and having the technical skill; it comes from the individual's mindset. This mindset comes from their beliefs, attitudes and behaviours. By paying attention to what goes on inside their head and ensuring that all their thoughts, attitudes and behaviours are positive and supportive, individuals can reach great heights in all their performances.

Winning Strategies outlines a systematic plan to help you develop and achieve peak levels of performance in your sport and your life. A combination of key skills, strategies, and techniques from life coaching, sports psychology, neuro linguistic programming, and hypnosis are included to help you take your performance to greater heights.

You can apply these skills, strategies and techniques to soar to new levels of achievement and satisfaction in your sporting life in order to raise your game and be the best you can be. Whether you want to achieve better results, feel more satisfied with what you do or go after that gold medal, this process will outline the steps to help you get there.

The *Winning Strategies* process is divided into sections starting with the foundation building areas (*Getting Started*) and then onto the specific performance enhancement skills, strategies and techniques (*Mental Preparation* and *Event Performance*) that will make a difference to how well you perform. The last section provides for continuous improvement to help you improve your performance for the next time around (*Post-Event Review*).

Many of the principles outlined in this book are based on neuro linguistic programming (NLP) approaches. Richard Bandler and John Grinder initially developed NLP in the early 1970s. The name NLP, according to O'Connor (2001) came from the three areas it brings together: neurology – related to the mind and how we think, linguistics – related to how we use language and how it affects us, and finally programming – related to how we sequence our actions to achieve our goals. Essentially, the language we use affects how we behave and we often behave and react in an automatic manner without thinking.

Initially, the idea behind NLP was to study how the best communicators communicate, not only through the words they used and also how they thought, felt and behaved when they were at their best. This then evolved into studying how others, who were excellent in their field, did what they did. In NLP terms, this was called modelling.

This *Winning Strategies* book is a form of modelling the processes that top sportspeople have used to achieve what they have achieved. It is also based on personal experience of working with clients as well as from a wide variety of sports psychology resources that I've come across in my years of practice. Yet, recognizing that every individual is different, you may find some of the elements described here as 'common sense' because you already perform some of the steps, whereas for others, it might be completely new.

All the elements here contribute towards achieving peak levels of performance, so whether you work through the chapters in sequence or dip in and out as need be, you can make a difference to your results and develop your own *Winning Strategies*.

So let us get started!

Getting Started

The aim of the **Getting Started** section is to provide the initial foundations for achieving peak performances. Whenever you decide you want to go after a particular goal, there are several elements that you can put into place to ensure outcomes that are more successful. Yet, much like building the foundations of a house, the stronger the foundations are, the stronger and more solid the house will be.

The first step towards achieving peak performance levels is to identify and clarify what it is you want to achieve. This **goal-setting** process is important because it provides you with a clear picture of the outcome you want to achieve and a clear direction to focus your energies and efforts. It also provides a way to measure and keep track of your successes. Once you have clarified the outcome you want to achieve, it is then important to explore your **motivation** – the reasons why you are doing it. The *why* of what you are going after will affect the amount of effort you put towards your goal and will influence your self-discipline to do what you need to do.

The next step towards achieving peak performances is to explore your **values and beliefs** associated with the goal. Achieving your goal and achieving peak performances becomes easy and effortless when your actions are aligned with your values. Your values are the core of what is important to you. By understanding your values, you can ensure that your goal for peak performance is aligned with what is important to you.

Your beliefs are how you view things, whether you think something is possible, real or not. Your beliefs may be positive and supportive or they may be negative and self-limiting. By exploring your beliefs, in particular identifying any limiting beliefs that might be holding you back or hindering your progress or performance, you can then replace them with empowering and positive ones.

Many of us have heavy demands on our time, energy and attention. These demands may be different if you are a professional athlete, a serious sports competitor or just want to realize your fullest potential; yet, there are still many demands from all your responsibilities and activities. The next step to explore in this foundation area is **self-management**. This is a step where you will explore those demands and explore what people, places and things fuel you or drain you. Once you have identified these, you can put in place strategies to maximize the positives and minimize the negatives to ensure you are fully energized for your performances.

The final foundation area is to ensure you have a good **life balance**. By taking a snapshot of all the important areas in your life, and by evaluating the time you actually give to those areas, you can then make adjustments to align your activities with your priorities. By being clear as to what is important to you and what your priorities are, you can use that information to determine whether your actions help you or distract you from achieving your goals.

Having these strong foundations in place, you can then go onto the specific mental skills and strategies to build a strong mental house.

Goals and Motivation

Excellence, in anything you do, comes from a commitment to yourself to go after your dreams. People who strive for excellence articulate a vision of where they want to go, what they want to achieve and clearly know the reasons why all this is important to them. They know what steps they need to take to get there and have milestone goals to mark their progress. They fine-tune their focus to ensure all their actions, their efforts and their lifestyle supports them in achieving the goal.

Successful individuals regularly set goals, align their activities towards that goal, monitor their progress on an ongoing basis, and make adjustments to ensure they are on track to achieve what they want to achieve. Locke, Shaw, Saari and Latham (1981, cited in Garratt, 1999) identify four benefits of goals. They say goals create focused attention, create energy, create long-term willingness to keep going, and create the opportunity for new learnings. Therefore, the benefits of clearly defining your goals can help to increase your performance, motivation, focus, discipline and confidence. The more precisely and positively you can define what you want, the more easily it will be to pursue your goal and therefore more likely you will achieve your goal.

Some people think of goal setting only in the context of big goals like buying a house, getting that new job, running a marathon, or qualifying at a certain level of competition. They identify what they want, make a plan of what to do, and then take action until they achieve what they want to achieve. You can also set goals, and gain the positive sense of achievement from smaller goals such as what you want to achieve in today's training session, tomorrow at work, or the DIY project at home this weekend. Goals might simply be what you want to do today, like simply get to the gym for a workout.

In the context of achieving peak performances, a more formal goal-setting process helps to provide structure, sequence, and a clear direction forward. This formal process helps you towards achieving peak levels of performance in everything you do. Yet, before you formally set those goals, you need to get clear on what it is you want to achieve.

START DREAMING

As children, we often dream of all the things we want to be, do, and have when we grow up. Yet, as we get older, we tend to 'get sensible', to 'get real' and forget about our dreams. It is from these dreams that great things can happen and great achievements attained! So, start dreaming! Let your imagination run wild with all the possibilities and allow yourself to have that childlike freedom with no limits or sense of what is achievable. By stretching your imagination of the endless possibilities, magic happens! Whether you wanted to become an Olympic athlete, be on a professional sports team or a national team, get onto the podium or simply complete your first and only marathon, take some time to recall the dreams that once fired up your imagination.

To help you fire up your imagination with some possibilities, ask yourself: *If you could be, do or have anything you wanted, and money was not an issue and failure was not a possibility, what would you be, do or have?*

I suggest you get a notebook or create a file on your computer or tablet for all the exercises and questions you will do as you read this book. It is important to take action, to write things down, rather than simply thinking of your answers. By writing things down, you make them that much more concrete and real, rather than a thought that simply comes and goes into thin air.

Let those dreams that you write down be as serious or as silly as you want! It is somewhere between having those dreams and your current situation where there is room to take steps towards making them a reality. When you create this dream list, it is not important *HOW* you will achieve these dreams, it is more important to get excited about the possibilities in the first instance.

If you are using this process with a particular performance in mind, start dreaming about how you want it to go, dream about all the great things that will happen and how amazing you will be. *From all these dreams you have written down, which one do you want to pursue right now? Which one do you want to turn into a goal and take action on? Which one do you want to take through this Winning Strategies process and achieve peak levels of performance?*

Within the context of goal setting, particularly with a sports goal, it is important to recognize the difference between outcome goals, performance goals and process goals. Bull (2006) explains these goals very simply, yet very effectively, in that outcome goals are the what, performance goals are the why and process goals are the how.

For example, an outcome goal might be to win a gold medal at the Olympics in the marathon; a performance goal might be to complete the marathon in

2h10m, and a process goal might be to run strong and maintain a consistent regular pace much like a metronome, and to remain mentally focused on the actual race.

You have complete control over process goals because they relate to how you will perform. However, the outcome and the performance goals may be influenced by outside things such as another competitor who is better on the day or the weather conditions that are more challenging than expected. Bull (2006) goes on to say by focusing on the process goal helps give us confidence and prevents us getting carried away with the intensity and pressure of the moment. Bull (2006, p. 56) states that by getting "the basic performance processes right, the outcome will look after itself". Essentially, by releasing the need to achieve a particular outcome and focus just on the process of how you can achieve it, you will get there in the end.

TAKING THOSE NEXT STEPS

Many of us simply dream about all the things we want to be, do and have. Yet, if we do not take any action, they remain simply dreams. So, action on your part is required to turn your dreams into reality! From your list of dreams that you have just written up, identify one that you are going to pursue.

To transform those dreams into reality, you need to create a more real and tangible image of what it is you want to get and to set some goals for yourself. Using the well formed outcome questions can help. Creating a 'well formed outcome' gives you a solid start and helps you on your way to peak performances.

The well formed outcome is based on the SMART goal setting formula; SMART is an acronym for specific, measureable, achievable, realistic and timely. The well formed outcome formula also includes additional questions using the PURE acronym as a reminder to state positively, under your control, right size and ecological. Effectively, to 'keep it real'.

SMART goals are based on the principles of Locke's goal setting theory (cited in Mind Tools 2013) and are a powerful way of motivating ourselves. Locke's research demonstrated a clear link between having a specific goal and an individual's performance. Individuals who only had vague goals did not perform as well.

The following well-formed outcome steps are based on Churches and Terry's (2007) questions and follow the lines of the SMART acronym. They then go to use the PURE perspective to further clarify what it is you want to achieve.

Answering the questions from each step will help you articulate the outcome you want to achieve. It is almost as if these questions can give you a rich and colourful 3D image of your goal rather than simply a flat 2D perspective.

Specific Simple	*What do you want to achieve? Where do you want to be at the end of the process or journey?*
Milestones Measurable	*What will be your smaller, milestone steps? How will you know when you achieved your goal? What evidence will you have?*
Achievable Attainable	*Do you have the resources to achieve your goal? Do you need to get additional support or resources to help you achieve your goal?*

Results Realistic	*Is the goal realistic and do you stand a good chance of achieving it?*
	Is your goal in line with your other priorities and objectives?
Timing	*When will it happen? What is the timescale?*

Now that you have written out your goal using the SMART formula, look at your outcome from a PURE perspective. These questions can help you verify your goal and help clarify things even further to create that rich 3D image.

Positive	Ensure that your goal is written down as a positive statement, as if you already have achieved it.
	If your goal is written down in a negative manner, ask yourself: *What do I want instead or what would happen if I could do something?*
Under your control	Check that you can take all the steps yourself, or that you have access to someone who can help you out, to achieve your outcome. *Do you need to request their involvement or secure their availability for a particular time or have them complete a particular task?*
Right size	*Is your goal the right size for you?* If you always achieve you goals, then make this one bigger. If you do not always achieve your goals, make this one smaller and more achievable.

Ecological	*What will be the effects on others when you achieve your outcome? Are there any unintended consequences, either negative or positive, of having this outcome?*

Look at all your answers now in light of the goal you want to achieve. *How does your goal appear to you now? Is it clearer, more attainable? Does it feels as if it is more real now?*

An example of a SMART and PURE goal using my first marathon is below.

Specific Simple	I want to complete the Ottawa Marathon in 2000.
Milestones Measurable	I will follow a training plan suggested by my club running coach for progression with my long runs in view of completing the marathon distance.
	The goal is measurable in that I can 'check off' the long runs completed.
	I can also measure my progress when I complete the half marathon in Brighton and by crossing the finish line in the Ottawa Marathon.
Achievable Attainable	Running the marathon distance is achievable and attainable regardless of the time it takes me to cross the finish line.
	I have all the resources to complete my training – running kit and shoes, advice from experienced runners and the time to do the training.

Additionally, as long as my health remains strong, and the means to return to Canada to run in Ottawa, I will be able to achieve the goal.

Results
Realistic

This goal is realistic in that as long as I focus simply on crossing that finish line, regardless of the time, I know I can put one foot in front of the other. Even if I have to walk parts of the course, I know I have the determination to carry on.

The goal is also in line with my desire to regain my physical health and all the training requires me to take extreme good care of my physical and mental well-being. If I do not take good care of myself, I would be unable to sustain all the training.

Timing

The race is 21 May 2000, and I intend to start training in December 1999. With five months of training, that is adequate time to develop the endurance to run the marathon distance of 26.2 miles.

Now, looking at the goal from a PURE perspective.

Positive

It is now 21 May 2000, and I have completed the Ottawa Marathon crossing the finish line.

Under your control

Yes, all the steps are within my control yet I value the input and advice from other experienced runners and coaches.

Right size	As I had never attempted a marathon distance, I did not know if it was the right size or not. I chose to believe that I could do it and would simply need to take my time.
Ecological	Yes, my goal is ecological and has no negative consequences on others. I am concerned about the impact on my physical health, yet with due care and attention, I aim to be all right.

Having written out your goal using the SMART formula and verified it from a PURE perspective, hopefully this will have fired you up ready to go! Even if you are totally enthused about your goal, your motivation can fluctuate, particularly when the going gets tough. Sometimes we just do not feel as if we have the energy to go out and do the things you need to do such as training because of busy schedules, other things to do or even the weather. Therefore, to help you increase your levels of motivation to keep yourself going, regardless of your goal, let us explore motivation in more detail.

MOTIVATION

Even if you are all fired up with enthusiasm to pursue your goal, you may have moments where your motivation may fluctuate between very high and very low. Yet, your level of motivation to pursue a dream will influence everything you do – from the time you put into preparing, to the self-discipline, to the actual effort on the day. Many gold-medal winners eat, sleep, and breathe their goal. They are aware that everything they do feeds directly into the results they achieve! If they do too much heavy training one day, they might not have the energy the next day. If they have a late night or do not eat healthy nutritious food, they may feel the impact on their efforts. Yet, we may not desire to be as regimented with our routines as others, regardless of the consequences.

Achieving some of your goals may require hard work on your part. Goals require a level of self-discipline and focus, and they may even require a certain level of commitment that affects other areas of your life. Jones and Moorhouse (2007) suggest that motivation is not just what drives us towards our goals, it is about our very existence and what we stand for; it is our reason for being. Therefore, knowing what your motivating factors are will help you do what needs to be done for you to achieve your goals. These motivating factors can act like magnets drawing you towards your goal, yet some motivating factors can drive you away from some place that is not comfortable and that you want to avoid.

Motivation taps into the reasons WHY you are doing what you are doing. Here are some questions to help you assess your motivation.

- *What are your reasons to pursue and achieve a particular goal?*
- *What will it mean to you to achieve the goal?*
- *What will happen when you get it?*
- *How will achieving this goal affect other aspects of your life?*
- *How is the outcome worth the time, effort and energy?*

Again, write down all these answers and take some time to reflect on them. *What do they mean to you?*

14

What is their significance? How can you use them to keep you motivated?

I know of some clients that actually post this list of reasons on their fridge, by their computer or even in a mirror that they look into every day. This helps to provide a very real, very physical, reminder as to why they are doing what they are doing. It acts as a reminder that all their time, energy and investment to what they are doing is worth it!

MOTIVATIONAL DRIVERS

Once you have reflected upon the reasons why you are pursuing a particular goal, here is something else to ponder – your motivating drivers. Exploring these drivers will help you clarify even more those reasons why, and, will increase your motivation levels even more. You may be internally or externally motivated and you may be motivated either moving *away from* or moving *towards* something.

Internal motivation comes from an individual's own sense of what they want to achieve and stems from their own personal value that they have attributed to something. Jones and Moorhouse (2007) suggest that internal motivation is based on a person's own value for personal growth and development as well as their desire for challenges to extend their capabilities. Overall, both parties state that internal motivation results in more enjoyment, less pressure and more effort such as longer hours and more dedication and commitment to their training.

External motivation drivers are derived from factors outside an individual and come from what an individual thinks others expect them to do or to achieve. A coach might set targets or even goals for you; they might require you to do extra training sessions or focus on

15

certain areas that you are not keen to pursue. Perhaps a parent has expectations of how their child can perform and pushes them to achieve those targets when in fact the child is not interested.

Let us take, for example, an individual who wants to improve their time in their next 10K race. Internal drivers might be that they want to see how much they can get out of themselves, how capable they are because they enjoy challenging themselves. External motivators might be that they want to prove to their coach, their friends or anyone else that they can do it. My internal driver to run the marathon was to prove to myself that I could do anything I put my mind to, yet there was also a bit of wanting to prove myself to others who doubted me!

Both internal and external motivation drivers provide incentives to individuals to improve their performances. Yet internal drivers are generally stronger and more powerful because we are doing something for ourselves. *Looking at your list of reasons why you want to do something, what are your drivers? Do your reasons why stem from your own measures of success or has someone else defined them for you? Are they internal or external drivers?* Remember, there is no right or wrong here. It is simply acknowledging the difference and ideally finding some drivers that are internal, rather than purely external ones.

In addition to internal and external motivating drivers, there are also *towards* or *away from* drivers. And again, there is no right or wrong here. It is simply that one is more powerful than another.

A *towards* motivator acts as a magnet drawing you towards the goal. An *away from* motivator acts as a repellent pushing you away from something. Effectively, a *towards* motivator is something that you want yet do not have. An *away from* motivator is something that you do not want yet you have. The *towards* driver has a stronger incentive to keep on going simply because you may get complacent with an away from motivator. When you move far enough away from an uncomfortable place and the pain and discomfort is no longer there, even if you have not achieved your goal yet, there is less incentive to continue on.

Let us take an example of an individual who wishes to achieve a specific weight target. Many individuals might relate to this in the fact that they have taken up running or exercise as a means to manage weight. A *towards* type of motivation would focus on all the benefits when that desired weight is achieved. This driver acts as a strong magnet drawing you towards those positive aspects you will get in your life when you achieve your goal. An *away from* type of motivation might be focused on losing a certain number of pounds. The person is not comfortable at their current weight and wants to lose a fixed number of pounds. Yet, when they move far enough away from the previous uncomfortable place even if they have not achieved their target weight, there is less discomfort. When there is less discomfort, there is less incentive to continue being vigilant and to maintain the new habits. Some old habits may creep back in!

So, what are your motivating drivers? Are they acting like magnets drawing you towards something positive, or are they acting like a repellent pushing you away from a situation you do not want? Many individuals have a long list of *away from* motivating drivers. They have more things they do not want, yet have, in their lives. So, to help turn these motivators into more powerful pulling magnets, try turning things around into something positive. Turn the negative 'do not want'

17

statements into positive 'want' statements. For example, let's say you have a few extra pounds of weight that you do not want. Creating a positive statement of wanting a slimmer, more toned, body would effectively mean the same thing as wanting to lose those pounds. Another example might be that you do not want to come last in the 10K race. By turning that into a positive statement you can congratulate yourself on simply completing the distance regardless of where you are placed. You could reassure yourself that you did it and a lot of people were not even participating and simply standing on the sidelines!

Overall, your levels of motivation to achieve a particular goal may fluctuate. However, by reminding yourself of what it is you want to achieve and why you want to achieve it will help you maintain high motivation! With high levels of motivation, you can achieve anything you set your mind to! Perhaps you could put all the reasons why you are doing what you are doing on sticky notes around where you live and where you look at regularly like the bathroom or bedroom mirrors, the fridge, or on the door as you go out each day. These reminders will help to keep at the forefront of your mind the reasons, the differences and the benefits that all the training and effort will make in your life!

Jones and Moorhouse (2007) outline the keys for optimal motivation. These include:

- Approach, rather than avoidance. Focus on what you want rather than what you do not want.
- Active, rather than passive. Make things happen rather than simply letting them happen.

- Do it for yourself, rather th?
  because you want to do it, ra?
  to please someone else.
- Positive, rather than negative. ᴗᴗ
  you enjoy what you are doing rather than ᴗᴗ
  of desperation.
- Internal, rather than external. Focus on doing
  it because it gives you a sense of both pride
  and achievement, rather than focusing on the
  outcome and its rewards.

MAKING A PLAN

After you have written out your goal using the well-formed outcomes questions and you are clear about your reasons why you are pursuing your goal, you need to make a plan of action.

You might start off by simply thinking about what you need to do, based on your own ideas and experiences. Then, you might look at others who have achieved a similar goal and find out what they did to achieve their goal. Once you have all the steps of what actions need to be taken, you can then develop a progressive plan of action. *What needs to happen first, and then after that, and then after that?*

Whatever format you use to plan how you are going to achieve your goals, the essential element of goal setting is that you clearly identify and write down what it is you want to achieve, by what date and how you are going to get there.

All the minute details of the 'how' that you will complete your plan is less important, at the initial stages, than getting it perfect. Just simply knowing that there is something you need to address and that you can clarify the details later is sufficient. The important thing is to

.ve a direction as to where you are going and what your nitial steps are. If you are unsure what your first steps are, ask a trusted friend, coach or mentor for their input. They might have some ideas as to the things you might consider and include in your plan.

For example, if you have a goal to complete a triathlon in the next year however the problem is that you are not a great swimmer, then perhaps you might pick an easy triathlon to complete, one that is friendly and easy for beginners. You might also consider taking some swimming lessons to improve your swimming as well as asking people who have done triathlons before for ideas on what they considered for their training. You could also find an easy training plan to follow or enlist the help of a coach to support you and devise a plan to suit your individual needs. Nutrition is something else to consider so that aspect needs to be explored in terms of what you need to take during the race to keep you going. All these things come from your own thoughts around your goal and what you need to do, as well as gleaning ideas from others.

Once you have a plan, even if it is a rough one, you can start taking action and make it happen!

SUMMARY

Goal setting is your first step towards achieving peak performances as it provides a direction to focus all your activities and your energy. Without a clear focus and direction for your actions, you may not achieve what you want to achieve. Although you may have an idea of what it is you want to go after and get, you may not be as effective or efficient in getting there. Clear goals help provide razor-sharp focus for your attention and help ensure your actions are on track to get you there.

The goal-setting process starts with choosing what it is you want to achieve. If you are unsure, then by activating your childlike mental muscle of all the things you want to be, do and have, you will start the creativity flowing. Then choose one of those dreams and turn it into reality! Using the SMART and PURE questions will help you become crystal clear as to what your goal is. By asking yourself the well formed outcome questions, you will get an almost 3D image of your goal.

Once you are clear on your goal, the next step is to make a plan of action. Breaking down a big goal into smaller milestone goals can help you to assess and measure your progress, and to take satisfaction that you are on your way to achieving your dreams! The subsequently identified minor goals are the mini steps that help you along the way and contribute (once achieved) towards a sense of achievement and progress towards your bigger goal.

With all this planning, it is also important to consider your motivation. These are the reasons why you want to achieve your goal and will be the force that pulls you along to help you do all that you need to do. Your motivation will influence how much effort, energy and self-discipline you apply towards achieving that goal. These motivators can act as an incentive to keep you going, even when the going gets tough. Wherever your motivation comes from, ensure it remains high so that you continue to take action until you achieve your goal.

Once you have clarified your goal and planned what you need to do, the second step in the mental peak performance process is to explore the values and beliefs related to your goal. This step further strengthens your motivators to achieve a particular goal.

STEPS SUMMARY

1. Decide on something you want to go after and pursue as a goal.

2. Write out your goal using the SMART and PURE questions.

3. Clarify the reasons 'why' you want to achieve your goal and the difference it will make to your life.

4. Identify the internal and external drivers and the *away from* and *towards* reasons to help create strong magnets to pull you forward.

5. Make a plan of action as to the steps you need to take.

MY JOURNEY

Once I proved to myself that I could complete the 10K race, I then decided to take on a bigger challenge. I set my sights on the Ottawa Marathon in May 2000 and started marathon training.

I sought help and advice from more experienced runners and did my research to find a balanced programme that would get me from complete beginner to completing a marathon. I was only interested in crossing the finish line, with a smile on my face, regardless of how long it took me! The incentive and motivation that kept me going was really and truly proving that I could do anything I wanted to do. Yet, there was some external motivation to prove to others who doubted I could actually 'do it', that I could!

Some thought I was a bit mad to even attempt to do all the training and actually run a marathon, particularly after I had been so ill. Yet, being somewhat

---

stubborn, I rose to the challenge. Coming back from being flat on my back and unable to eat to completing a marathon in less than one year would be something I knew I could call upon in future to remind myself of how far I had come. And, remind myself of how much I can do when I put my mind to it!

GOALS AND MOTIVATION

24

Values and Beliefs

The next step in your winning strategy formula is to identify the values and beliefs related to your goal. Values are the core of what you do and what is important to you. Loehr and Schwartz (2003) say values are a road map for action and that they fuel the energy on which purpose is built. When your actions are aligned with your core values, achieving your goal and achieving peak performances becomes effortless.

Your values are what makes up the core of who you are and what you stand for. You may even get fired up if your values are not respect or challenged. This might mean you feel tension, frustration even aggravation when your values are not respected.

Your beliefs are your filters of how you see the world and these may change over time and depend on circumstances. At one moment you may believe something is true and then the next moment, you have new information and you believe something else is true. When exploring beliefs, it is important to acknowledge that your beliefs may support you and empower you, and they may also limit you and hamper you.

For example, when I was recovering from my illness, I did not believe I could run a 10K race let alone a marathon. Yet, I had not even tried running that distance and had no basis of evidence for that belief. That was my limiting belief and I was challenged by my friend Lloyd to believe, at least as a remote possibility, that I might be able to complete the distance. I came to believe that I could indeed put one foot in front of the other, regardless of how fast or slow I ran, for 26.2 miles – the marathon distance.

You might wonder how values and beliefs relate to developing a winning strategy and achieving peak performances. Well, when your actions and activities are aligned with your core values of what you consider as important, all your efforts and your results become easy. If you value, for instance, good health and vitality, then it will be easier to eat well and exercise. Contrarily, if you do not value, for example, personal challenge and being the best you can be, you may not push yourself as hard to train or to achieve the results you say you want to achieve.

Also, if you do not believe you can actually achieve the goal you set for yourself, you actually limit your potential. Yet, if you can remain open and receptive to the possibility that you can achieve it, you may just achieve it! Therefore, exploring your beliefs can help you identify and banish any negative or limiting beliefs as well as ensuring that your beliefs, in regards to you achieving your goal, are all positive and supportive.

VALUES ... WHERE DO THEY COME FROM?

Your values are the fundamental core of what is important to you and how you live your life. Your values are generally adopted from the important people in your life while you were growing up. These influential people might have been your parents, your family, your teachers or even your peers. Whatever they deemed as important, you most likely have similar view on what is important to you. Occasionally, we may hold radically different values from our parents and authoritative figures. Yet for the most part, they are pretty similar.

Values might include such things as respect for self and others, honesty, love, and holding yourself accountable for your actions rather than blaming others. Values could include the value of peace, fun and adventure, stretching your comfort zones or staying within your comfort zones, being the best you can be or just doing enough to get by. More examples of core values might include such things as excellence in everything you do, service and contribution, and making a difference.

The list is endless and a key question to ask yourself is: *'What is important about what I do?'* In regards to your goal that you are using with this Winning Strategies process, ask yourself, *'What is important about achieving this goal? And, what else is important?'*

When you start asking yourself these questions, some of the values of 'what is important' might be easy to think of. However, keep on going and keep on asking yourself the question *'What else is important to me?'* Even after you think you have exhausted all ideas, ask yourself the question again and see what else reveals itself.

Attempt to get as many values as possible. Aim to write down at least 10 values of what is important. If you can get more, that is great! Just keep on writing down whatever comes to mind and see what comes up. Regarding your goal, you might come up with things like wanting to be the best you can be, wanting to challenge yourself, or wanting to realize your potential. You might even value the thought of being an Olympian or playing in a national team or even travelling the world representing your country. Perhaps you value the fame, the fortune or the money. There is no judgement about what your values are because they are uniquely yours.

After you have written out your values in regards to your Winning Strategies goal, you could also look at each important area of your life and ask yourself what is important about that area. You might discover that you have similar values in these important areas and they are called your core values. Core values are those values that are common to all areas for your life. For me, one of my core values is self-care. This developed particularly after I had been ill and was unable to do literally anything until I got better and healthier. Yet, there have been times since then that I have not made self-care a priority such as when I have worked too hard or continued training even when I was injured. Yet overall, it is a priority and I do take good care of myself by eating well, resting sufficiently and taking time out for me before I do anything else. This just helps me to be more effective when I do everything else.

With the knowledge and insight into what is really important to you, you can then ensure your activities are aligned with those values. In turn, this alignment helps you to focus your energy along the lines of who you are and what you are all about.

MORE HELP WITH IDENTIFYING YOUR VALUES

Over the years of working with clients, I have a few more questions to help you explore your values rather than simply ask *'What is important?'* about something. Why not take some time to read each question and write down in your journal or document the answers that come up for you. You might be surprised at the greater insight you gain for yourself.

- What would you say are your personal character strengths?
- Who are you when you are at your best? What qualities are evident?

- Imagine you are at your 100th birthday party with friends, family and colleagues. Everyone is standing up talking about what a difference you have made to their lives. What stories would they tell?
- When you sit quietly after this 100th birthday party and reflect upon your life and all the stories that were said, what would you say are the three most important lessons you learned about life and why are they so significant?
- Think of several (at least three) individuals that you admire and respect. You may know these people personally or simply from their public presence. What are the top three qualities about each individual that you admire and respect the most?

These questions are to help you create a richer image of who you are as an individual and what is important to you. Take some time to reflect on your answers, and from there, you might more easily identify with values that are important to you. *What do the answers to those questions say about you? What core values can you draw from the answers?*

By thinking about the impact and contribution you have had on other's lives and the lessons you have learnt throughout life, you might clarify elements of what makes you uniquely you. This uniqueness might be demonstrated through the fact that you 'walk your talk' and live your life according to what is truly important to you.

By reflecting upon other individuals you have admired and respected and by identifying the qualities that you like so much, might help you to see the qualities that you yourself have, or would like to develop.

Now that you have a clearer picture of what is important to you in regards to your goal, the next step is to prioritize those values. Knowing which values are the most important to you, you can then use this to evaluate everything you do and align your actions to match up with your values. To complete the ranking of your values, review all the values you identified and ask yourself, *'Which is the most important to me? If I could only have one value met, which one value would that be?'*

After you have identified your most important value, continue to rank the remaining values. Continue to ask yourself, *'If I had the previous value met, and could only have one more value, what would that one value be?'* Ranking your values can then help you to assess all what you do and align your actions with your values.

ALIGNING ACTIONS WITH YOUR VALUES

Now that you have completed this ranking process of your values and you are clearer on what is important to you, you can then compare your actions with those values more easily.

For example, my two top values include self-care and being the best that I can be. Yet, there have been times over the years where I have continued to exercise and to train when the little niggle that I was choosing to ignore, turned into an injury. On one occasion, it even resulted in me having to seek urgent medical attention because I could not move!

I certainly was not demonstrating good self-care by ignoring the pain and I certainly was not being the best

I could be when I persisted with the running even though I knew I had an injury. Had I been aware of my values at that time, I might have realized that my actions were not in alignment with my values and stopped what I was doing. These days, I am more aware of my values and whether or not my actions are aligned.

Are your actions and activities aligned with what is truly important to you? Is there anything you could change or modify to ensure a better alignment between your actions and activities, and your values? Are you doing anything that has little or no bearing on what is truly important to you?

You could use this prioritized list of values almost like a checklist for everything you do. You can compare your actions with what is on the list to determine whether you are being true to yourself, and in being true, what is important to you. When there is a difference between your actions and activities, and your values, an internal conflict arises. This internal conflict can create tension that in turn negatively affects you and your ability to be the best you can be.

I recognize that when I became ill, I was not living my life according to my value of self-care and well-being. I was unhappy in my job and was effectively running away all the time or keeping myself so busy that I didn't have time to stop and think about my situation. Even though I valued taking care of myself by eating well and going to the gym, I really was not looking after myself very well. Finally, after the conflict had gone on for a period of time, my body gave up and became so ill that I had to take notice.

A conflict between your values and your actions or activities will cause negative stress, tension and even, at an extreme, injury or illness. This internal conflict can easily drain you of your energy, your strength and even your motivation, which in turn will affect everything you do in so many areas of your life.

To illustrate this point, a common situation I see with clients is that they value their family more than their sport. They feel it is important to spend quality time with the family. Yet conflict arises when they are devoting more time to their training and less time with their family. Another conflict arises when there is a race on the same day as an important family obligation. Someone who is very clear on the priority of their values, and valuing family before sport, the internal struggle as to the best decision to make is over very quickly. Family is more important so they go to the family thing and comfort themselves in the fact that there will be other races to participate in.

When you experience conflicts between your actions and your values, there is some internal tension whether you are consciously aware of it or not and it does affect your performance abilities. Sometimes, we can benefit from having an external person such as a trusted friend or coach to help 'hold up the mirror' so that we can clearly see those conflicts.

Once you have completed this identification of what your values are and are clear as to their priority, let us go on to explore your beliefs.

BELIEFS ... EMPOWERING AND DISEMPOWERING

Your beliefs are how you view the world and therefore how you act and react within your environment. It is important to recognize that these beliefs are viewed through your own personal filters whereby you may delete, distort, or generalise what you see and how you see things. We all have different filters based on our experiences. Lazarus (2006, p. 82) says beliefs "tend to be generalisations, in other words how we have generalised certain events and assumed they are truths". Yet the key difference is whether these beliefs are helpful to us or not. Generally, beliefs are about ourselves, about our abilities and about other people and things outside of us.

You can have positive and empowering beliefs that open you up to the possibilities of limitless potential. In the sporting world, world records in every sport are being smashed all the time. What previously was thought as impossible has become possible. Therefore, by being open and receptive to the possibilities, you enable yourself to expand your potential. Take for example the previously held belief that man could not run faster than a four-minute mile and everyone accepted it without question. However, you now know it is not true, that that belief was unfounded. At the time, before Roger Bannister broke the four-minute mile barrier, people did not even question things any differently; they simply took it as fact.

However, some beliefs may actually not help you be the best you can be. They might even hold you back and set a ceiling on what can be achieved. They limit your potential and are referred to as limiting beliefs. Limiting beliefs might include such things as 'I'm not good enough', 'I couldn't possibly do that' or even 'It's too hard'. Some negative, limiting, beliefs might even be beliefs that are deep-rooted where you might not even be aware that they are having an effect on your actions.

In order to achieve peak performance levels, it is essential to explore your beliefs about what you do to ensure that you are open to the possibility of achieving your potential, and dispel any limiting beliefs that may hold you back.

To help you identify some of your beliefs, here are some opening statements to get you going on some global beliefs. Global beliefs are broad, general statements regarding yourself, your life, your relationships, your work, your friends, and everything you do. Some of these global belief statements might start with:

> I am …
>
> People are …
>
> Life is …
>
> The world is …
>
> I can't …
>
> People should / shouldn't …
>
> Women / Men are …
>
> Change is …
>
> The future is …

You also have some 'if/then' beliefs. These beliefs are based on 'if' something happens, 'then' something else always happens … which is the consequence of the 'if'. Some examples include:

> If you believe in yourself, you can do anything.
>
> If you trust people, they take advantage of you.
>
> If a particular competitor shows up, then you don't have a chance of winning.
>
> If the other team score first, then you will lose the match.
>
> If you can get through this next mile, then you can finish the whole marathon.

So, *what are some of your beliefs about your goal?*

Write these beliefs down to be able to more easily examine them. Once you have written down your beliefs, you need to examine them to determine whether they are empowering or disempowering. While examining them, ask yourself, *'If I believed this, how would I feel and is there any evidence that makes it true?'* If you feel good about the belief, then it is likely that it is a positive and empowering belief. If you do not feel so good about yourself nor do you have any evidence, then it is likely that it is a negative limiting one.

Garratt (1999) provides an excellent exercise to help identify and then dispel limiting beliefs. For this exercise, you need to complete each sentence with whatever thoughts come to mind. For example, think about when you lack confidence, when you want to have confidence and how it will be when you do have that confidence. The answers may be revealing and help you to dispel any limiting beliefs.

Step 1 – I **lack confidence** when … (insert where and when you lack confidence) …

> because …
>
> before …
>
> after …
>
> while …
>
> whenever …
>
> so that …
>
> if …
>
> although …
>
> in the same way that …

35

Step 2 – I **want to have confidence** when … (insert when you want to have confidence)

> because …
>
> before …
>
> after …
>
> while …
>
> whenever …
>
> so that …
>
> if …
>
> although …
>
> in the same way that …

Step 3 – I **will be confident** when (insert when you want to have confidence)

> because …
>
> before …
>
> after …
>
> while …
>
> whenever …
>
> so that …
>
> if …
>
> although …
>
> in the same way that …

The answers to those questions can then guide you to take action such as discarding limiting beliefs and taking action to help y o u focus on the empowering beliefs. By answering these statements, you shift from a mindset of where you lack confidence, have hope for when you will have confidence and then move into a place where you do indeed have that confidence.

Often, your limiting beliefs have come from well-intentioned authoritative figures that you have adopted. You have simply taken them as fact. However, if you have no proof about the validity of a belief, then discard it or transform it into an empowering belief. Replacing a limiting belief with an empowering belief is similar to asking yourself the question *'What else could I believe that would be more helpful to me in this situation?'*

SUMMARY

Identifying your values and your beliefs in relation to your goal will help you towards achieving your best ever performance. Having that strong connection to what is truly important to you helps boost you up for achieving amazing possibilities. Then knowing what is important to you and why it is important can help you to ensure that you align your actions to support you in achieving your goal. If something is worth enough and important enough, then you will most likely do whatever is necessary to get you there in the end.

Part of aligning your actions with your values is to prioritize your values in an order of importance. That way, if there are any conflicts affecting your ability to achieve your goal, you will clearly see what might be slowing you down or stopping you towards your goal achievement.

Furthermore, understanding what your beliefs are, particularly in relation to your goal and what you need to believe in order to achieve that goal, can help strengthen the possibility of actually achieving what you want to achieve. Identifying your beliefs might also uncover some limiting beliefs that could be holding you back from actually achieving what you want to achieve. Ensuring that all your beliefs help you along the way and support you in achieving your goal, fosters a greater connection to actually achieving the desired outcome.

This connection of knowing what is important to you and ensuring that your beliefs support you in what you are going to do also contributes to your sense of self- esteem and confidence in yourself. This in turn positively contributes towards your ability to perform at peak levels.

STEPS SUMMARY

1. Identify your core values related to your goal.

2. Prioritize these values.

3. Align actions with values, and make any adjustments as necessary.

4. Identify all beliefs related to your goal achievement.

5. Transform any limiting beliefs

MY JOURNEY

Once I h a d decided I was going to prepare for and run a marathon, the reason why it was so important to me was first of all because it gave me a legitimate 'excuse' to take care of myself. I needed something outside of myself to help motivate me to take care of me. Re-joining the human race and simply being a productive member of society was not enough incentive to 'take care of me'; I wanted to prove something more to myself. Marathon training meant for me that I had to eat healthy and nourishing foods, avoid all alcohol, and get plenty of rest. It was the excuse I needed to stay on the 'straight and narrow'.

I also wanted to prove something. I wanted to prove to myself that I could do it, that I could have the dedication and discipline to tackle a challenge that I thought was previously beyond my reach.

I most certainly did have beliefs that limited me! I did not believe I could run (or even walk) a 10K race, let alone a marathon distance. The reason I had this belief was because I had no real conception of how far it actually was and no idea as to how long it might take. I simply assumed that I could not do it because I had never really run any distances before.

Left to my own devices, I would never have attempted it simply because I did not think it was possible. I was challenged to dispel that belief, one step at a time. With each long Sunday run along the Brighton and Hove seafront and on the South Downs, I proved to myself that I was doing distances I had never dreamed I could do. And, if I could do those distances, what reason could I give for not doing the marathon distance. I could find no valid reason!

Self Management

Managing ourselves and all that we have to do, and want to do, can be challenging. Yet, if you are already a busy person, you most likely already have pretty good time management skills and ideas as to what your priorities are. Yet, it never hurts to brush up on them to see if you can refresh your memory of some good strategies to implement and see where you can make a few improvements.

In addition to the traditional time management strategies, there are also energy management strategies that can make a difference. One way to look at your energy management is to look at the effects of people, places and things on how you feel and their effects on your energy levels. You can develop attitudes and approaches to those people, places and things to minimize what drains you and maximize what fuels you. This can help to ensure your energy levels are as high as can be for when you need it the most, for example, on the day of your big performance.

Additionally, in light of effective self-management, you can also look at your energy systems from a different perspective to develop strategies to ensure your fuel levels are topped up for those key performance times. According to Loehr and Schwartz (2003), these energy systems run on physical, emotional, mental and spiritual fuel. To be fully engaged and perform optimally, you need to be physically energized, emotionally connected, mentally focused, and spiritually aligned. We will explore these fuel systems to help you to become fully engaged for peak performances.

MANAGING YOURSELF AND YOUR TIME

There are many books, articles and courses on effective time management to help improve effectiveness and productivity. It all comes down to a few simple, yet not necessarily easy, principles to follow. These principles include identifying what you have to do, knowing what your priorities are, having a schedule for when you are going to do it and finally keeping focus to ensure you actually take the necessary action.

For many of us, in addition to focusing, for example on preparing for a big race where we want to do well, we also juggle the responsibilities of life. These might include work, family, children, and community involvement, and the list can go on. By actually writing down all your activities and responsibilities, including what you need to do for your Winning Strategies goal achievement, you will more easily be able to prioritize your activities, create boundaries between activities and do what you need to get done.

So, take a moment now to write out all of these roles and responsibilities that you perform on a regular basis. Then, decide what is important to do and where you have flexibility. Important roles and responsibilities might include taking care of the children, going to work at a regular set time and even training every day.

The next step is to decide whether you can fit all of these roles and responsibilities into a weekly schedule, so it's time to create a weekly schedule. This weekly schedule helps you to have some structure in your week and it helps to ensure you have time and space to do all the things you want to do, and need to do. It can be easy to think that you will go to the gym so many times a week, do technical skills and drills training, do some stretching and flexibility exercises, do some mental skills sessions ... and all this on top of your work and your family responsibilities. If you do not know when specifically you will do something, it might not ever happen. So, that is why a timetable is helpful.

By inserting all the roles and responsibility into your timetable, or even in your diary, you have to consciously make the decision to shift an activity somewhere else if you decide that you just cannot make time for it. If the activity was not in the diary, and only just a thought of something to do or an intention, then it is easier to let it slip and not do it.

Writing out this weekly schedule can be challenging in terms of fitting everything in. It is when you literally see on paper (or on the computer screen) that you have a lot to do and a lot to fit into your schedule that you may realize some difficult decisions m a y need to be made.

If this is your situation, where you have 'too much to do and not enough time to do it', then look at the list of all your roles, responsibilities and activities and review what can be either delegated to someone else, supported by someone else, or put off until after your big event.

The first step in writing down your weekly schedule is to put in all the activities that are immoveable – those where you do not have flexibility such as work, regular commitments or group training sessions. Next, put in all the activities starting from the top of your priority list onwards. For anything you cannot fit into the schedule on a regular basis, ask yourself whether you could put them off until after the big performance event.

Sometimes when a particular goal is very important to us, we have to make some adjustments in our lives to accommodate the time necessary to do all the preparation. This might mean that certain activities are postponed or certain tasks either delegated to someone else or put off until after your event. This enables you to keep your eye on the ball and focus.

To illustrate these time management principles, here is an example for a triathlete who wants to qualify for their age group and compete at the World Triathlon Championships.

Step 1 - List all the activities
In the first instance, simply list all the activities as they come to mind.

- Work (Monday to Friday, 9 a.m.–5 p.m., with occasional late nights)
- Family time with partner and children (every evening for at least an hour)
- Parents – weekly visits with parents
- Household chores (usually once a week for cleaning and grocery shopping)
- Triathlon training (2 x swim, bike and run, strength and flexibility training)
- Yoga class – minimum once, if not twice, a week
- Meditation class – once a week
- Friends – socializing once week
- Toastmasters Club – a public speaking club which meets twice a month

Step 2 - Prioritize the activities from most important to least important

This priority order may be based on what is important to you, and how important the triathlon goal fits into the big picture. If you cannot fit everything into your weekly schedule, this will help you see what you can put off until a later day.

- Work (Monday to Friday, 9 a.m.–5 p.m., with occasional late nights)
- Family time with partner and children (every evening for at least an hour)
- Triathlon training (2 x swim, bike and run, strength and flexibility training)
- Household chores (usually once a week for cleaning and grocery shopping)

- Yoga class – minimum once, if not twice, a week
- Parents – weekly visits with parents
- Meditation class – once a week
- Friends – socializing once week
- Toastmasters Club – a public speaking club which meets twice a month

The first four activities are essential and must be done, whereas the remainder of the list are nice to do however not critical in order to do the necessary training to qualify. These non-critical activities might be put off until after the qualifying races for the World Championships.

You might also consider spelling out exactly what training you need to do, and whether that training is done on your own (and therefore you have flexibility when it can be actioned) or with a group such as a club training session where you do not have flexibility in regards to the timing of the session.

Once you have identified the priority activities, the next step is to draft a weekly timetable.

Step 3 - Draft up a weekly timetable

This is where you draft a timetable to include those things that are immoveable and where you do not have any flexibility, and those activities and times where you do have flexibility.

	Sun	Mon	Tues	Wed	Thurs	Fri	Sat
6 a.m.		Rest	Swim	Bike	Run	Club Swim	
9 a.m.	Club Run	Work	Work	Work	Work	Work	Club Bike
12 p.m.	Family	Work	Work	Work	Work	Work	
3 p.m.	Family	Work	Work	Work	Work	Work	Chores
6 p.m.		Family	Family	Family	Family	Yoga	
9 p.m.		Medi-tate		Medi-tate		Family	Medi-tate

Although seeing friends and going to the Toastmasters Club is fun and is part of your regular routine, during the intensive time preparing to qualify as an age-grouper in triathlon, these extra activities can be done when time permits or resumed after the qualifying races.

Leaving some empty spaces in the diary allows you the flexibility to add in the extra activities such as seeing friends or activities that you have not made a priority for the duration of the training.

This weekly schedule can be used as a guideline to follow. It does not necessary have to be 'set in stone' and followed rigidly if you do not want it to, yet, it shows you where you actually have spaces in your schedule to do all that you do want to do.

Once you have a weekly schedule you can follow, you can then move on to looking at your personal energy management.

PERSONAL ENERGY MANAGEMENT

Every activity you do in life takes 'energy'. Energy is expended when you get up in the morning, when you prepare and then eat your breakfast, when you brush your teeth, when you travel to work, while you are work ... and the list goes on. Can you recall a time when you were at home feeling unwell with something like a cold? Then, when you started to feel better and decided to return to work or normal activities, you found you didn't feel so well again. This is because simply getting up, getting dressed and going about your regular normal day were taxing your weakened energy. You may have felt fine at home, yet when you have expended more energy to get into work and be on form, you may not feel as strong.

Let us look at another example such as when you develop a new skill or new habit. At the beginning, it takes a lot more energy while you are learning and less energy once you have mastered the skill. *How many of you can relate to when you first started driving a car? How stressful and tiring were those first few times driving?* If you are like most people, you were quite nervous and there seemed to be so many different things you had to pay attention to at once. It might have even been a nerve-racking experience for fear of missing something important. However, once you mastered the skill, you were able to drive without any worries. What about when you get up and go to work on a regular day versus when you have to go in early for something. *Do you sleep as well as you normally sleep when your routine is disrupted?*

In terms of energy, when you were learning the new skill, the amount of energy required was probably very high and you might even have felt tired or exhausted at the end. Whereas, once you mastered the skill and did not have to consciously think about all the little things, the new skill did not take as much energy. Within the context of a performance event such as a sporting competition, you can become so practiced at what you are going to do so that you do not have to think that much about all the required steps. Much like getting up and going to work, the same amount of energy can be expended in the lead up to your performance.

Another way to think about energy is to recall a time when you were with a friend who was negative and pessimistic. *How did you feel afterwards? How did you feel after spending time with someone who is positive and optimistic? Does one particular person leave you feeling tired and drained, and the other leave you feeling buoyant and uplifted?*

Developing an awareness of the people, places, and things that drain your energy as well as energize you, can help you in the context of performance because you can develop strategies to ensure that your energy levels are as high as they can possibly be before a big performance event.

According to Richardson (2000), the key to effective personal energy management is to know what replenishes your energy and what drains your energy. Not only is it important to understand the concept of energy management in your day-to-day life where you can put in place activities that regularly replenish yourself, it is also important when you are gearing up for a big performance.

Bigger and more important events will place greater demands on your energy levels. Depending on what type of athlete you are, these events will vary. For a recreational athlete, simply going to a competitive event will be stressful and more demanding on their energy levels. For an Olympic level athlete, it might be going to an international competition or even the Olympics that places greater demands on their energy. It is important to recognize that the performance event can be very literally something that requires physical effort, as well as anything that may be mentally demanding. Anything that places a demand on your energy system will have an impact on your energy levels.

Additionally, your energy levels are influenced by your approach and your attitude about the task in hand. *Recall a time when you were looking forward to some sort of activity. How did you feel? What about a time when you were dreading something? How did you feel then?* Oftentimes, the excitement can buoy you up while the dread of something will drain you. *What differences did you notice between when you were looking forward to something and when you were not? What were your energy levels like?* These insights can help you when you look at the people, places and things that fuel you and that drain you.

WHAT FUELS YOU AND WHAT DRAINS YOU?

Go back to your list of activities you have just drawn up about where you spend your time. Now look at that same list and ask yourself how much energy you expend on each activity. Also include the people you spend time with. Give a subjective rating to each person, place and thing you come into contact with, basing this on how much energy (high, medium or low) a particular person, place or thing has for you. *Do you feel drained or do you feel buoyed by the activities you do and the people you are with?*

Positive energy activities are those activities that make you feel good, vibrant, energized and recharged. This might include spending time with special people (including yourself) or doing things you love and enjoy. For example, the Sunday runs, although physically draining can give you positive energy because of the 'feel-good factor' of completing them!

Negative energy activities are those activities that drain you of your energy and could make you feel negative, down or drained. This could be anything from being unhappy or discontent with a particular situation, concern and worry over someone close to you, a disorganised office or a complaining friend. Sometimes even just dwelling on an unresourceful situation can be a negative energy activity.

Remember to include the people and the places, in addition to the activities. For some, being in a big city surrounded by a concrete jungle or being around people who are negative and pessimistic might drain them. However, for others, being in the country or going for walks by the seaside might replenish their energy.

Having insight into the different people, places and things that drain your energy and those that fuel you up over the course of a typical week, you can then identify what adjustments you could make. These adjustments will help you to ensure that you have peak energy levels when you need and want them most.

For example, certain activities at work make me feel full of energy and I love doing them, whereas other activities (like bookkeeping and accounting) I do not like. When I have to do my monthly accounts, I often feel tired and drained. Therefore, it makes me wonder whether it would be worth my while to delegate this particular responsibility to someone else.

Another example is doing housework. I know many people hate doing these types of chores yet I love it. I put music on and dance around my place as I'm doing the household chores. I always feel good about doing the chores because it's a time to actually listen to some good music while getting a job done that does not require me to engage my brain. Plus, I feel proud to have a 'nice shiny and clean place' to live.

For other people, just getting to the gym is a struggle, yet when they actually complete their workout, they feel energized. They have moved their body around, they have got their circulation going and they may even feel more mentally strong and powerful. As this activity refuels their energy levels, it is something they might consider doing when their energy levels are low.

Once you have identified the activities that fuel you and those that drain you, you can then do something about it to ensure you minimize the negative impact and influence of those people, places and things that drain you, and ... maximize the positives. Here are some food for thought questions to help you come up with ideas on how to minimize the effect of those activities that drain you, and do more of those activities that fuel you.

For those activities that drain you:

- *Can you avoid them altogether? Can you get any assistance to complete them or delegate them to someone else?*
- *Can you reduce the length of time you are exposed to the draining people, places, or things?*
- *If you have to be exposed to the drainers, what different approach or attitude could you have to help minimize the draining effect?*
- *What things are you procrastinating about doing or making decisions about? What can you do now to get moving on them?*
- *Who can work with you to lessen the impact of any negative drains? Can you get someone to help you out?*

For those activities that recharge you:

- *How can you incorporate some sort of recharging activity into every day?*
- *What mechanisms need to be put in place so you can do what you need to do?*
- *What can you do that will help you feel more positive and recharged in just a few minutes?*
- *How often do you need regular recharging sessions such as a weekend away, a holiday or even a day off?*
- *How can you spend more time with those who make you feel good?*

ENERGY SYSTEMS

Let us imagine for a moment an electrical gadget such as a mobile phone that needs to be recharged on a regular basis so that it can do the job it is designed to do. Well, human beings also need a recharging element in order to function and this needs to be recharged on a regular basis as well. There is no specific place in the body where the recharge element resides, nor can you plug yourself into a mains electricity socket to recharge. You can however manage your energy levels to ensure they are high by surrounding yourself and doing activities that energize you. Yet, there are energy systems that you can effectively 'plug yourself into' to refuel and re-energize. Loehr and Schwartz (2003) explored these energy systems in depth within a performance context. These are your physical, emotional, mental, and spiritual energy.

Many athletes recognize the importance of taking care of their physical body. If they did not take care of their body, they simply could not perform to their optimum levels. You need to balance how much energy you expend with how much energy you renew almost like a simple in-out formula. If you expend a lot of energy, then you may need to rest for an equal amount of energy. This means that in order to do all the physical effort you require for your sport, you need to rest and recover. You need to feed your body with nourishing foods, drink sufficient water or fluids and get sufficient rest through downtime and sleep.

On an emotional level, you need to be able to do things that make you feel good about yourself and about your life. You need to enjoy what you are doing both for the sport that you are doing and the goals you are pursuing. This energy source is also feeling good about the rest of your life and what you do outside the training arena. You need to be able to put things into a positive light and take the good things from each training session and competition in order to learn and grow. This is where self-confidence and your sense of 'feel- good' about life come into play. You can

53

renew this energy through your relationship with yourself and others. When you feel good, you will perform at higher levels. When you are not feeling great about yourself or what you are doing, or perhaps are feeling stressed, then your performances will be less than your optimum.

On a mental side, this is where your focus, positive self-talk, optimism, and mental preparation come into play. This is also where you need to have a strong clear focus on where you are going and ensure that everything you do helps rather than hinders your ability to achieve your goal. Everything you do, in every aspect of your life, has an impact on your performance abilities. Every training session you do helps to build your strength, skills, and abilities to do your sport. Plus, everything you do outside the training arena will also have an impact. For example, if you have a stressful day in the office or at home and feel exhausted, how will your training session go in the evening? Most likely, it will not go so well and you perform poorly. Another example is if you went out and ate some unhealthy food for lunch, foods high in fats or sugars. How will your training go afterwards? Again, most likely, it will not be at the same levels as when you have eaten healthy foods. This demonstrates the direct link between what you do beforehand and its effect on your performance levels. Therefore, when you want to achieve peak levels of performance, you need to ensure that everything you do supports you, nourishes you and helps you to be the best you can be.

The spiritual source of energy relates to your own sense of connection with what you are doing and why you are doing it. It touches on your passion, courage, integrity and the meaning of what you are doing. It also touches on the community with which you connect. This is where your character, passion, and commitment come into play and make a difference to all that you do. *Ask yourself, 'What really matters to me and what difference is my connection with what I am doing going to make to my life now, and in the future?'* Refuelling this energy source by connecting with your sense of purpose and the reasons why you are doing what you are doing will fill up those energy tanks. By reminding yourself of your values and beliefs of who you are as a person and as an athlete will help as well as your connection.

By recharging and refuelling all four sources of energy, you can help yourself to be physically energized, emotionally connected, mentally focused, and spiritually aligned, and help take your performances to those winning levels.

SUMMARY

Managing your time and managing your energy are essential for your everyday life, and for helping you to achieve peak levels for performances. Putting into place effective time management strategies can help you ensure that you do all the things that are required to help you prepare as well as see what things that might be put on a back burner for a while until after the event. A weekly schedule provides a structure that helps guide you and remind you of all the things you need to do, and when you plan to do them. Some people may follow this schedule rigidly while others may use is as a guideline, yet what it ultimately does is provide a sense of structure and a tool which will help you complete all the things you need and want to do.

By appreciating the fact that everything you do in life takes a certain amount of energy and by putting into place effective energy strategies, you help yourself to have the n e c e s s a r y energy available to be able to achieve peak performance levels whenever you want or need to. Being aware that different people, places and things will either drain your energy or refuel you, gives you the information you need to do something about it! You can then put into place strategies to minimize those energy drains and maximize the positive energy gains. This is particularly important leading up to and including your big event where you need to have as much energy as possible. Ideally, you will avoid altogether anything that might drain your energy. Additionally, you will want to make sure you are surrounded with positive and energizing people, places and things so that you are brimming with energy for your event!

By paying attention to the physical, emotional, mental and spiritual energy systems, you can help yourself to be fully charged up to perform at your best. Simple actions each day to make deposits into these energy systems will make a difference to how you feel about yourself, about life and about what you need to do to perform at your best. By ensuring that all systems are fully topped up and charged up, you help yourself perform to the best of your abilities.

STEPS SUMMARY

1. Put in place a structured schedule to include all the things you need to do to prepare. Include the 'immoveable' activities where you have no flexibility as to when they happen and then slot in the activities that are more flexible and can be done when you make the time.

2. Identify the people, places and things that replenish your energy, and those that drain your energy.

3. Decide on ways that you can minimize the situations that drain you, and maximise those that energize you.

4. Come up with ways you can replenish your physical, emotional, mental and spiritual fuel tanks.

MY JOURNEY

The concept of self-management and my own energy systems became crucial to me during my recovery because my energy was so weak. Simply getting up out of bed and going to work took a lot out of me energy-wise. Plus, if something happened that stressed me, I would almost immediately lose energy. I had daily routines that I needed to stick to almost rigidly in order to simply survive, function and work. Any deviation from that routine would negatively impact on my energy.

At that point, many acquaintances thought I was a bit mad to even contemplate training for a marathon. They very reasonably thought that all the running and training would have a negative impact on my energy. The running and training did drain me, which as a result, made me limit any other activities in order to protect what energy I had left. It also gave me the perfect excuse to take afternoon naps, to have a sleep and restore my energy after those long runs!

There were times when I would be out socializing with friends in the evening and then all of a sudden, I would feel weak and have no energy. Nothing particularly stressful happened; it was just my body's way of saying that it needed to go home and rest! Unfortunately, when those moments hit me, I had to leave immediately. Not five or ten minutes later – it was there and then! My abrupt departures did not go

---

down so well with some people; however, that is what I felt I needed to do in order to survive!

I also became acutely aware of what people, places and things drained my energy and replenished my energy. The impact on my ability to sustain just normal day-to-day living activities was influenced by those things that drained me. I therefore had to become very guarded about who I spent time with, what activities I did and where I would go … all in view of surrounding myself with positive people who helped boost my energy rather than drain it.

Life Balance

In today's busy society many of you are rushing from one thing to the next and complain that you have too much to do and not enough time to do it in. This may leave you stressed, strained, or irritable. Even if you are focused on doing whatever is necessary for your performance and even if you have clear boundaries about when you will and will not do things, you may still feel a pull from all the other things in your life. You might have noticed this when you did the weekly schedule of all your roles, responsibilities and activities in the previous chapter about Self Management.

It can sometimes be challenging to juggle all the competing demands on your time and your energy. To help you be as effective as you possibly can be, you benefit from identifying what is important to you, what your priorities are and then ensure that all what you do is aligned with those priorities. This is summed up succinctly by Butler and Hope (1995) as spending your time doing those things you value or that helps you to achieve your goals. Both stress the importance of knowing what your values and your goals are. Furthermore, knowing what your priorities are and how they are aligned with your actual activities is the key to peak performance. Your priority might be to be the best you can be in your sport, in your professional life or in your personal life. Whatever the case, living life in a more balanced manner will definitely help you along the way.

So, what does it mean to live life in a balanced fashion? For some, it may mean doing everything at work and everything at home before the end of the day. For others, it means having the time and energy to spend on what is important. Whatever definition you use, living your life in balance contributes to healthy physical and mental well-being. This in turn helps you to be the best you can be and contributes towards achieving peak performance levels.

UNBALANCED LIFESTYLE

During this exploration of living life in a more balanced manner and all the benefits you will gain, it is important to highlight some of the negative effects of not having a healthy balance. Everyone is different and everyone will be affected to varying degrees; however, when we go about our life in an unhealthy manner, there is an impact not only on our health, but also on our productivity and our performance. Unhealthy lifestyles can be anything from not getting enough sleep, not eating healthy foods, not moving the body or exercising adequately to excessive alcohol intake or use of other unhealthy substances.

The negative effects of not living a balanced lifestyle include:

- Increased stress and irritability
- Decline in physical and mental health
- Low job satisfaction and morale
- Reduced productivity
- Increased rate of errors and accidents

One of the biggest consequences of living your life in an unhealthy and unbalanced manner is that your energy is drained. When you have less energy, you are less effective and cannot perform to peak levels.

Sometimes challenging decisions need to be made to lead a more balanced life and the question is simply whether you are willing to make those decisions, and accept the consequences, in order to achieve what you want to achieve. For example, if you want to take your sports performances to higher levels, you might not be able to continue partying every weekend or you might need to cut back on your weekend socializing. Another example might be if you spend less time at work because you want to train for a sporting event. Whatever choices you make, make them consciously and know what the impact they have on the rest of your life.

BENEFITS

Although it is important to recognize the negative effects of living life in an unbalanced or unhealthy manner, let us focus rather on the benefits you will gain. These include:

- Physical and mental well-being because you are recognizing what is important to you and taking action.
- Energy and vitality because you are recharging your physical and emotional 'batteries' regularly.
- Enthusiasm and motivation because you are spending time on what's really important to you.
- Effectiveness and efficiency because you become more focused on what you do and when you do it.
- Success and satisfaction because you are clear about what you are doing and where you are going.

Recognizing the benefits of achieving a better balance is one thing; doing something about it is another thing! This is easier said than done!

My definition of life balance is living your life in a manner that you do what is important to you and spend sufficient amount of time on the priorities in your life. It boils down to living your life by design and with a sense of purpose and direction, rather than by default, according to someone else's purpose and desires. Through living your life in a healthier balanced manner, you become more focused. Your attention and your energy are on what is important to you. Within the context of peak performances, you can direct that attention and energy towards ensuring that all that you do supports you in being the best you can be.

By identifying what is important to you, you can align your activities with these important areas and then evaluate all what you do to ensure you spend time on what is important and on what helps you to be the best you can be. Similar to knowing what your values are, as we discussed in the Values and Beliefs chapter, you can evaluate everything you do in line with the important areas in your life. If, upon examination, you determine that a particular activity or project does not positively contribute towards you achieving what is important and achieving your goal, then perhaps it would be wise to not undertake the project in the first place or to let it go. Alternately, you could make a conscious decision to put the project on a back burner while you focus on things that are more important and when the time is right, you can pick the project up again.

IDENTIFYING WHAT'S IMPORTANT

Asking yourself what is important in your life can be a serious revelation for some people. So, let us explore a 'Wheel of Life' exercise step by step. According to Mind Tools (2013), "The Wheel of Life (or Life Wheel) can help. Commonly used by professional life coaches, it helps you consider each area of your life in turn and assess what's off balance. Therefore, it helps you identify areas that need more attention". Effectively, this exercise helps you to take a snapshot of what is important and a graphical representation of how satisfied you are in each area. From this starting point, you may then choose to focus on improving one area over another, depending on your focus and your goals.

Some ideas of important areas in people's lives include:

Health / well-being

Finances / security

Work / career

Fitness / sports

Children / partner / friends

Recreation / fun

Religion / spirituality

Community / personal development

Travel / adventure

Everyone is different as to what categories they have. For some individuals such as keen sportspeople, their sport endeavours are a separate and distinct category, whereas for other individuals they might include their physical activities in the health and well-being category. You decide the categories that fit for you and the above suggestions are simply food for thought. To help you identify these important areas, ask yourself, '*What defines me as a person and what is important to me?*' You might even consider the particular goal where you want to be the best you can be as a separate category.

To provide a graphical representation of the important areas in your life, draw a circle and then divide the circle into 8 slices. Enter the important areas, the categories, of your life into each of the segments. You might have fewer than eight and that is fine.

Having identified the important areas of your life, the next step is taking a snapshot of how you feel in regards to each area. On a scale of 1 to 5, rate your current level of satisfaction for each important area, with 1 being unsatisfied to 5 being satisfied. Then draw a line across each segment at an approximate point to represent your satisfaction level. Zero is the very centre of the circle and 5 is at the outer rim. An example of a blank Wheel of Life is below. You add the heading in terms of what is important to you and then place a line across the spoke of the wheel for how satisfied you are.

Figure 1 : Wheel of Life Template

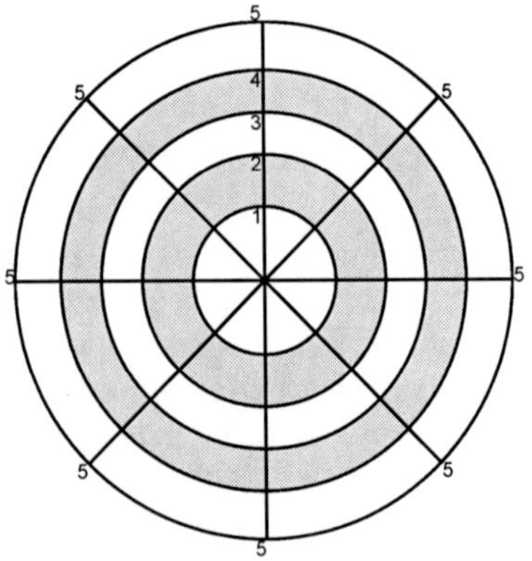

Once you have completed the wheel with the important areas and rated your level of satisfaction, take a step back and ask yourself, *'What does my Wheel of Life look like? If the lines across each segment were the outer rims of a wheel, how smooth would my ride be?'* A completed Wheel of Life can be an eye-opener because many of us are indeed having a bumpy ride! So, *what changes could you make, what small steps could you take, to move your current satisfaction level in one or several of the areas?*

It is one thing to be aware that the ride is not as smooth as you might like it to be; yet it is another thing to take action. Therefore, you need to decide on small steps you can take to shift your current ratings to something more positive. By proactively taking action and doing something to move yourself forward towards becoming more satisfied, there is a positive cascading effect in other areas of your life. Much like a ripple on a pond – when you start to feel more positive about one area in your life, you begin to feel better about other areas. Subsequently, when you feel better about things, taking action in those other areas becomes easier!

ACTUALLY MAKING THOSE CHANGES

The information and insight you gain from completing this Wheel of Life exercise will help you to then make any adjustments so you can live your life in a more balanced manner. In an ideal world, we would all spend adequate time on the important areas. However, more often than not, there is a conflict. We spend more time on less important things and in order to lead a more balanced life, something has to shift. When we focus on what is truly important to us, this often helps us feel happier and more contented and as a result, we become more productive in what we do – be that in sports or in life.

What changes can you make to help you move towards a better balance? Do you need to spend more time on certain areas? Less time on others? Can you involve others to help you out?

Some changes are simply a matter of 'just doing it' - making a decision and then implementing it. However, other changes require the consent, support or involvement of other people. Perhaps you need to review your working hours with your boss so you can get to the training sessions with the club. Perhaps you need to swap child minding with a friend so you can get out for your run or go training. Perhaps you need to put off the project at home to renovate until a later date. *Could you reduce the time you spend on some, less important, activities and increase the time on other, more important, ones?*

To help you get that balance right for you, here are some more questions to consider:

- *What needs to change to make this better? List all possible changes.*
- *Who can make these changes? Identify the changes that you have control over, and those that someone else controls.*
- *For those changes within your control, list the steps you need to take to achieve your changes, along with a timetable for taking action.*
- *For those changes that someone influences, make your request along with the benefits for them to help you.*
- *What needs to be put in place for these changes to work? Any support or assistance from others?*

The answers to those questions can provide you with some stark insights into yourself and you can then make some decisions about how and where you want to place your time, attention and energy. *What changes can you make to create a better balance? What actions will you actually take and what support mechanisms need to be in place for you to take those actions?*

LIFE BALANCE AND PERFORMANCE

You may be wondering what the connection is between having a balanced life and performance. Well, this is similar to the connection between values and beliefs and your actions. If your actions are not aligned with your values and beliefs then there is a conflict. If there is a conflict, then it will negatively affect you, your energy and ultimately your ability to be the best you can be.

In regards to life balance, if you want to be a top-class athlete or simply reach your full potential, you need to make sure that you place the necessary attention to those priority areas. Yet, if there is one area in your life that may be dragging you down and bothering you, or if you are concerned or worried about a particular area that is not going so well, it will indeed affect your ability to perform. When we are pre-occupied with other things, your levels of energy will be affected and your ability to place your attention on what you need to do to perform is compromised.

Sometimes we do need to place certain things on the back burner while we focus on a different priority for a while. Or, perhaps there are certain steps that we can take that redress the balance while we still continue to focus our energy and our attention on doing whatever is needed to prepare for and perform to the best of our abilities.

Take for instance when I trained for that first marathon after I had been ill. I placed all my attention on my work and my training, to the exclusion of my friends and socializing. In a certain way, I thought I was being 'selfish' in a self-preservation kind of way. Although I thought that was what I needed to do, it did however cost me a relationship. So in hindsight, perhaps I could have eased up on my intense focus of my training and spent a bit more time with that person and with friends.

SUMMARY

Living life in a more balanced way helps you to realize peak performances because you are focusing your energy and your efforts on what is most important to you, yet still maintaining a balance with things. We are all different and it is important to recognize when looking at your personal life balance, what may be a balanced life for you might be very different from what a balanced life is for someone else. Everyone is different and we may all have different views and definitions of what living a balanced life means. Others may not agree with you, yet, you may need to take into consideration their views before deciding for yourself what works best for you.

By completing the Wheel of Life exercise and rating your satisfaction levels, you can see whether, overall, you are having a smooth or bumpy ride. This may highlight some areas that you have been neglecting and that perhaps paying some attention to them might help you feel good about yourself, and as a result, positively impact on your performance abilities.

Ultimately, if you want to be the best you can be, you have to be clear on what is important and ensure you devote sufficient time, energy and attention to preparing. As a result, you may need to put some projects or activities on the back burner for another day, possibly after your big event. Yet, just be mindful of what you are doing and the impact it may have on others around you.

STEPS SUMMARY

1. Identify the important areas of your life on the Wheel of Life and then rate your satisfaction levels.

2. Decide what actions you can take to increase your satisfaction level in all that is important to you.

3. Decide whether you are comfortable leaving some areas untouched or whether you devote less time and attention for the period while you are preparing for you big event.

4. Monitor your progress and make any necessary adjustments to ensure you stay focused and on track towards achieving your goal.

MY JOURNEY

While I was recovering from my illness, my top priority was of course regaining my physical health because I knew that without it, I would be unable to do anything else. I knew I needed to work in order to pay the bills so being healthy enough to sustain a normal working day was paramount. The ability to train and run was secondary.

Yet, because I was so determined to do the running, my life revolved around ensuring that my body was nourished and rested sufficiently in order to sustain the training. There was not much else in my life to juggle other than eat, rest, work and run!

Initially, during the early stages of my recovery, I had very little energy for much else other than work and light training. So, socializing with friends was almost non-existent! Also, if I ate unhealthy foods or drank any alcohol, it was as if my body was already struggling enough simply to stay upright and 'function' normally with work demands so any extra strain on the system tipped me over the edge and I could not handle it. I would become very weak, lose my energy and sometimes have to lie down and rest until I was able to be upright again.

I had been in a relationship before I became ill, and the person was very supportive. However, the strain of my narrow focus during this time took its toll. When we were out with friends during my recovery period, I would suddenly feel like I had no energy left and that I needed to get home to rest. These requests to leave immediately took their toll and we eventually went our separate ways.

I continued to maintain a narrow focus on work and training right up until I did the actual big run – the Ottawa Marathon in 2000.

Mental Preparation

The next area in the Winning Strategies process is **Mental Preparation.** These steps provide you with performance enhancing tools and techniques to take your performances from good to great and then to outstanding! These next steps deal specifically with your mind, your thinking, and your attitude and can positively influence any performance.

These skills include developing rock solid **confidence** levels in what you are about to do. You can work on strengthening your confidence just as you would work on and strengthen any other muscle in the body. Your self-confidence does have an effect on your abilities and the outcomes you achieve. If you have doubts or lack confidence, your performance will suffer. Therefore, by building up your confidence levels, you can raise your game and improve your performance.

Another performance-related skill is dealing with your **internal dialogue**. This inner voice talks to us all the time. Whether you actually pay attention to it, or not, is another thing. That inner voice is sometimes positive and supportive and at other times it can be critical and destructive, much like your beliefs about what you can and cannot do. By becoming more aware of your own internal dialogue, you can then develop the skill to notice any negative or unhelpful commentary and turn the volume down. Additionally, by turning up the volume from your positive and supportive internal cheerleader, you can help yourself perform even better.

Finally, developing your **mental rehearsal** skills will be the difference that makes the difference. Mental

71

rehearsal, also called visualisation, is one of the most powerful skills you can master. Mental rehearsal is similar to watching a movie where you are the actor, as well as being the director. By imagining how you will perform on that crucial day, you are pre-programming yourself for success and the ability to handle any difficulties that may arise. Repeated mental rehearsal strengthens your ability to be the best you can be on the day since you have already gone through possible scenarios, at least in your mind, and dealt with things in a successful manner.

All of these mental preparation skills can be practised and honed before you arrive at your actual big event. This practice, much like putting those hours in the gym and the time practicing your particular skill, will stand you in good stead when you actually get to the event.

So let us get going and flex some mental muscles to help you on the day of your actual performance event.

Confidence

Many of us may have strong confidence levels in one area of our life yet not in other areas. You might be surprised by the fact that although you may think someone appears to be very confident simply in the manner that they walk and talk or perhaps because of how successful they have been, they might actually not have all that much confidence. They might simply be 'acting as if' they have the confidence, yet do not genuinely feel it or believe it. Yet, in all likelihood, they do have some confidence in some areas of their life. And, we can carry over these feelings of confidence from one area to another to help us strengthen our overall confidence levels.

Imagine this … you are calmly standing at the start line, focusing on what you are about to do. You know that you have done all that training and now it is simply a matter of that gun going off and you are on your way. You are bursting with confidence and are excited about the challenge you are about to take on. *Can you really imagine this, or, is your reality more that you are a jumble of nerves and having doubts and fears about your ability to do what you are about to do? Are you shaking your head as if saying, 'No way, I'm not ready for this' or 'I haven't done enough preparation and cannot do this'?*

Well, we all have moments where we have doubts, fears and feel nervous about what we are about to do. Yet, you can banish those doubts, fears and nerves by strengthening your 'confidence muscle'.

What Is Confidence

Confidence is the belief in yourself to do what you want to do; it is the self-assurance that you are capable and prepared to take on the task or challenge you have set yourself up for; it is the certitude that you can do it – whatever 'it' may be. It is based on experiences and your perception of how you measure up against your own 'measures of success'. This is how you define success, rather than how other people define it for you.

People with confidence have a 'can do' attitude and focus on the positives. They look for something positive, even when there does not seem to be many positives. An athlete will be calm and assured that they have done the training they needed to do and know they will do the best they can on the day, regardless of the outcome. They can be quietly confident that they can do the job at hand.

A confident person will admit when they make mistakes and will learn from them. Someone who is not so confident may beat themselves up for 'not being good enough' and not even entertain what they could do differently the next time.

Effectively, confidence is a by-product from things you do to reaffirm that you can in fact do something and do it well. Much like having good health is a by-product of eating well, drinking sufficient fluids, getting enough sleep, exercising and handling stress effectively.

You can also see confidence in a person in an almost tangible and real way. Whether the person actually feels confident or not may be different, yet from the outside they do look confident. Think about a time when you were speaking with someone who had their shoulders hunched over, their eyes downcast and spoke in a low voice. *Did they give you the impression they were confident?* Most likely not! However, if you think of speaking with a person who stood tall and straight, who had good eye contact and spoke with a clear strong voice, you might make the assumption that they were confident. Even if they were not feeling confident, they were acting as if they were confident!

CONFIDENCE … WHERE DOES IT ALL COME FROM?

Many factors and influences contribute towards your levels of confidence in what you do. This might include your family, friends, coaches, teachers, colleagues and bosses, among many others. Anyone who may have had an impact, either directly or indirectly, on your development as a person will influence the degree of confidence you have. Orlick (1998, p.54) suggests, "confidence comes from embracing the childlike qualities of positive vision, being absorbed in a task, and having persistence – especially for staying positive."

We develop our confidence based on feedback – be that from what we do and the results we achieve as well as what others say to us. Having confidence in yourself contributes to you feeling good about what you are about to do, to you having the expectation that you can perform to your current ability and to achieve what you are setting out to achieve.

Your confidence may be somewhat shaky due to uncertainty. Such circumstances might include times when you are put into a new situation that is unfamiliar to you, where you do not know exactly what is expected of you, where you are not 100% certain of the rules and you are with unfamiliar people.

Take for example when you start practising a new sport. Your confidence levels may not be very high because you do not know what to do or how to do it. You might feel intimidated by others on the team because they have more experience than you and you might even think of them as better than you. You might not know the best way to train, what to eat or how much rest you should be getting. All this uncertainty and insecurity contributes to lack of confidence.

Now, take another example where you have been doing something for quite some time. You know the rules, you know the players and you know what to do. You might even take some new participants under your wing, give them encouragement, tips and hints based on your experiences. This certainty of what you are doing demonstrates a confident you.

More often than not, our confidence fluctuates, and if we happen to have particularly low confidence levels right at the same time as a big event, it will impact negatively on our performance abilities.

CONFIDENCE AND PERFORMANCE

You may have ups and downs with confidence levels and this might be as a result of stretching your comfort zones because you are involved with something new or simply having a rough patch where you are not doing as well as you would like. However, the stronger your confidence muscle is, the more easily you can ride the waves.

Just to help you have a greater appreciation of how confidence levels can affect sportspeople's performance abilities, let us take a look at how this might show up when they are about to perform – be that in a sporting arena, a business arena or a personal arena. Some common indicators where a lack of confidence shows up include:

- They are never fully prepared – they could have always done with another week or match under their belt before they feel they are ready
- They are scared of taking a risk in case they fail
- They are thinking negatively and doubt their own talents and ability as they perform their sport
- They feel that they are not good enough
- They often lose concentration and do not focus on the job at hand
- They do not have a game plan or they have one yet do not carry it out

Recognizing how this lack of confidence might manifest itself is one thing, and it is another thing to really appreciate how it affects you in being the best you can be. *If you can think of areas where your confidence levels are not as strong as you would like, how does this manifest with you in your world?*

It is almost as if these low confidence levels weaken the physical body, a n d sets you up for making mistakes. Much like a self-fulfilling prophecy when you think it is going to go poorly, and then it actually does.

By taking time to investigate your thoughts and fears about what you are about to do and then examine them, you can then dispel the doubts. You could ask yourself whether there is any basis for such thoughts and fears, whether they are grounded in fact or fiction, or whether they a r e simply a generalisation with no real basis. If there is no basis or grounding, then simply discard them. If there is some basis, ask yourself, *'What can I do to minimize any negative impact?'*

Why not look at different arenas in your life. *Where do you have good confidence levels? Where are you less confident?* Write these down and see if you can pinpoint the different areas where your confidence levels vary. By noticing the different areas where you have more or less confidence, you can then easily start taking steps towards developing your own self-confidence workout and strengthening your confidence muscle.

STRENGTHENING YOUR CONFIDENCE

Orlick (1998) suggests the way to strengthen your confidence is by staying positive with yourself, finding reasons to believe and finding means to bring out the best in yourself. By remembering, thinking and looking for the positives on a regular basis in all areas of your life, you increase your overall sense of confidence in yourself.

Confidence comes from looking at the good things, all the things you did well and all the things that went right. Remember all the comments made by others that were like a pat on the back and acknowledged the good things you did. Confidence comes from knowing, and accepting that you will be good enough regardless of the outcome. Think what it might be like if you simply freed up yourself to live and perform to your greatest potential. *What would being free from the shackles of negativity and doubt be like?* When you focus on the negatives, you are almost giving yourself permission to perform poorly. You have a list of excuses to let yourself 'off the hook' just in case you do not achieve the expected outcomes. This negative focus can then become a habit that inhibits your performance abilities. So, focus on the positives. And finally, look for examples that demonstrate your value and your good efforts. Sometimes putting things into a different perspective can shed some positive light on things.

Like any other habit you want to change, it takes conscious and consistent effort to make those changes. Rather than paying attention to the worst-case scenarios and the negatives, choose to focus on the best-case scenarios and the positives. Become aware of your thoughts, become aware of where you place your attention, and become aware of what you focus on. Every time you notice you are thinking of something negative, shift your thoughts to something more positive which can help uplift you and your performances.

You can also work the 'confidence muscle' just like you would when you go to the gym to strengthen your physical muscles, with regular focused exercises. To help you get a sense of your own confidence muscle, try this exercise. Imagine right now that you are overflowing with supreme confidence. You are standing that bit taller, speaking out with more conviction and pursuing those things you would have only toyed with beforehand. *How does that feel within you?*

If you find this exercise is challenging because you do not know what confidence might feel like, think about someone whom you admire and who has confidence. *What sort of things do they do? What sort of things do they say? How do they hold themselves?* Then, imagine you are that person, doing what they are doing, saying what they are saying, holding yourself as they would. Act 'as if' you are that person. Step into their shoes and imagine taking on the same level of confidence they have.

With this level of confidence, either from your own experience or imagined from someone else, take a moment to think about how you might do things differently in any given situation. Get a sense of how easily and effortlessly things flow and how you interact with others. By tapping into this sense of confidence, whether it is real or imagined, you are starting to strengthen that confidence muscle. With repeated workouts, you will strengthen your confidence muscle even more.

Continue flexing those muscles and try another exercise. For this exercise, reflect on recent successes or times when things went well. *What things contributed to your success? What factors made a difference?* Take for example your last sporting event that went well. Some factors might include your training had gone well, you felt well rested and had eaten nourishing foods; it was a bright sunny day and the racecourse was flat. You might have been feeling good about yourself because something positive happened at work or at home.

Now, just for comparison, think back to an event when things did not go well. *What elements contributed to this experience?* Perhaps your training had been inconsistent, you were feeling run down and poorly, and you were feeling distracted by a problem elsewhere. *What is the difference between these two scenarios of when things went well and when things did not go so well?*

For example, some factors that create a good performance for you might be that you were well rested on the day, the weather was nice, you had done all the necessary training, and even things at work and at home had been going well. In terms of a poor performance, although your training and preparation had gone well, perhaps you didn't get a good night's sleep the night before the event or you had been feeling somewhat stressed about a work situation.

After you have written your answers for good performances and poor performances, take a step back to notice what you notice. *What are the key differences between the performances? Can you minimize or eliminate any factors that contributed to poor performances and ensure that you do indeed do all the things the same when you had good performances?*

This type of exercise helps you to create your own model of excellence, your own 'recipe for success' of all the things that contribute to your good performances. Then you will know what to do in future to h a v e a repeat of a good performance. Over time and with practice, you can add to and adjust your model of excellence to refine the elements and guarantee that if you do everything that you need to do, your performances will be great.

WRITE A CONFIDENCE RESUMÉ

Another exercise to strengthen that 'confidence muscle' is by writing a 'confidence resumé'. This is a list of all your achievements and successes – in all areas of your life – much like a training diary of your exercise sessions or a work resumé of all the jobs you have held.

This resumé helps you to focus on what you have accomplished, what achievements you have made and the successes that followed. Look for occasions where you stretched yourself and where you can give yourself a pat on the back. It may also include the small achievements, the minute details that make a difference or some other aspect where you can say, 'Well done me!'

This confidence resumé is a great way to acknowledge all the fantastic things you have done in your life and will help you to shift your focus onto the positives. *When you look at that list, how does that make*

81

you feel? Does it give you a sense of pride that you have indeed done some pretty amazing things? How are your confidence levels now?

Another technique you can use to help boost your confidence is to create an anchor. O'Connor (2001) says anchors are any stimulus that evokes a response. Anchors change our state and can occur naturally or are set up intentionally. *Can you recall hearing a particular song that makes you think of a special occasion? How about a particular sight or smell? Do they sometimes bring back memories and feelings? How many of you react, positively or negatively, to a raised eyebrow or a simple look over the rim of someone's glasses?*

Those songs, sights, smells, words or gestures are anchors. These anchors trigger stored thoughts, memories and feelings. Often anchors are set up unconsciously and you react to them without being aware of what is happening. You can, however, intentionally set up anchors to trigger specific thoughts, feelings, and states. The anchors become directly linked to a trigger gesture or image and the visualised states, such as confidence.

For some athletes, they link a sense of confidence to a memory or a photo of a great race where they were feeling strong, powerful and confident. Perhaps this photo is of them as they crossed the finish line or had a silly grin holding their medal. For others, they keep on recalling, with vivid sensations, what it feels like to be incredibly confident and then anchor that to a trigger gesture such as making a strong fist or holding their thumb and forefinger together. Simply by recalling that image of the photo, recalling that particular race or doing that trigger gesture, helps them to tap into those confident feelings.

Once those confident feelings are tapped into, you can then carry on as if you had all that confidence.

Now, practise recalling the trigger that gives you that confident feeling. Keep on repeating this exercise and recalling the trigger so that you are able to feel that sense of confidence easily and effortlessly. For me, my confidence anchor is a strong powerful fist where I feel a surge of energy and confidence travel through my hand, my forearm, my shoulder and then my chest. With that feeling of confidence in my chest, I stand that much taller. I look that much brighter and I confidently proceed with what I am about to do – be that in a sporting context or elsewhere in life.

On a final note, you decide what works best for you. Some people prefer recalling an image or photo while others prefer doing a trigger gesture. The key is to practise the trigger often so that you feel those feelings of confidence and can call upon it easily and effortlessly when you need it the most. Overall, play around with the different exercises to boost your confidence and see what works best for you.

DEALING WITH SETBACKS

I do not believe that a chapter on confidence would be complete without any mention of setbacks. We all experience setbacks from time to time and these can have an impact on our confidence levels. Setbacks can happen when you do not achieve the result you expected. This in turn can lower your belief that you can do whatever you set your mind to, and as a result, dent your confidence levels. Other setbacks might include getting injured and being unable to train or compete in that big race that you have been aiming for.

When you are not experiencing the results you want, it is important to put things into perspective. *Have you done all the training you needed to do? Have you been distracted by other more important things in your life, perhaps something much more important than what is going on in your performance arena?* In the grand scheme of life, sometimes there are events that take precedence over your preparation and you need to put them all into the melting pot that contributes to your performance results. These important things might include a major project at work for an important client, a change in personal circumstances, and major disruption to your routines or even a serious illness of someone close to you.

When you do have a setback, take some time to step back and view the situation in a more objective perspective. This may take a while to allow your emotions to settle down. Seeing the big picture of everything going on can help you pinpoint what happened and what affected your ability to be the best you could be. Maybe there was something going on in your life, maybe you did not do the training you could have done, or maybe you became distracted by priorities that are more important. Whatever the case, after objectively looking at the factors that affected your performance, decide whether there is anything you could do differently the next time.

When you are training and competing, sometimes injuries happen and that can prove to be a major setback. No one likes to be injured and sidelined when they are aiming for a big competition or want to achieve an important goal! Yet, having the ability to review and revise your goals, to do whatever is necessary to strengthen the injury and resume training safely will help you to come back even stronger than before.

This mental resilience to bounce back after setbacks and to remain positive regardless of the situation will help you become a strong athlete both on and off the field. You will more easily be able to deal with mistakes or when things are not going according to your plan. The key to mental resilience is your ability to stay calm under pressure and deal with stress. You need to stay strong in your self-belief that you can do what you set out to do, make your motivation work for you, and maintain focus on what you need to do and what you can control. According to the American Psychological Association (2013), some of the keys to developing mental resilience include:

- **Avoid seeing crises as insurmountable problems**. You cannot change what has happened, yet you do have control over how you react after a crisis has happened.
- **Move towards your goals**. Continue to do whatever you can towards reaching your goals, even if they are small steps towards ultimately getting you back on track for another goal.
- **Keep things in perspective**. Consider what is happening and keep the bigger picture and long-term goals in sight rather than blowing the situation out of proportion.
- **Maintain a hopeful outlook**. Keep an optimistic outlook that the situation will improve rather than worrying or being fearful about things and the future.
- **Take care of yourself**. Even though you may face a challenging situation, nurture yourself and be kind to yourself.

Although you cannot 'undo' an injury, there is most likely a means to repair the damage, even if it takes months of rehabilitation and physiotherapy. There is a way back, yet you may need to revise your previous goal. Do what you can to help yourself recover and take small steps that help you, such as doing those physiotherapy exercises every day. There will always be other races and events in which to participate. Even though you may have been in the best possible shape to do amazingly well, you can recover, one day at a time, and get back on your feet. Avoid spending lots of time and energy worrying about what could be. Simply stay focused on what you can do today to help remain hopeful of what you can do tomorrow. Even if you have to revise your goal, you can still continue onwards and remember that is it progress, not perfection. Above all else, make sure you take care of yourself and be gentle, acknowledging the small steps you make and know that you are making progress.

SUMMARY

Confidence is just like a muscle that can be developed and strengthened through repeated attention and effort. Yet recognize that your confidence levels may vary depending on the circumstances and may vary at different times. You can however strengthen your 'confidence muscle' so that you always have strong confidence levels whenever and wherever you are.

By finding reasons to believe in yourself and focusing on the positives, you help yourself shift into a more confident mind set. There are several exercises that help strengthen that 'confidence muscle', including writing a confidence resumé to remind you of all the good things you have achieved and done in the past. This can provide the boost you need to enhance your performance before a race.

The anchoring technique can create a direct link between a unique trigger gesture or thought and the feelings of confidence. Then, all you need to do is remember to use the trigger, and the feelings linked to it will be fired up. Confidence is a mind set and a habit. Therefore, with conscious and consistent efforts to strengthen that 'confidence muscle', you can soar with confidence at all your performances.

However, there may be times, such as when you are injured, that you have a setback and your confidence levels plummet. Therefore, you need to be good to yourself and put the injury and how it impacts on your life at the moment, into the bigger picture of life. Then, by doing what you can control such as regular daily physiotherapy exercises or by taking small, perhaps different, steps towards your goal, you will eventually get there in the end. You may need to revise your original goal depending on your situation, yet you can still compete again ... it might just be a different race or in a different arena.

STEPS SUMMARY

1. Identify a situation where you had good confidence levels and low confidence levels, and ascertain what contributed to these levels. Add this to your own model of excellence of what helps you to perform well.

2. Write a confidence resumé of all the situations where you had good confidence levels and where you felt good.

3. Develop a confidence 'anchor' to use when you want instant access to those same feelings.

4. Put things into perspective when you have any setbacks and see things from a big picture perspective.

MY JOURNEY

My confidence levels and my ability to run a marathon were pretty low to say the least. I did not believe I could do it and had no frame of reference really to relate it to because I had never done that kind of distance before.

Yet, with each long Sunday run whereby I was running distances I could never have even imagined myself doing previously, my confidence did grow. I also examined 'how far I had come' since being so ill.

When I did start eating again, and it was staying in my stomach, I recalled how I had to lie down after eating food. It was as if my body could not process the food in my stomach and keep me upright. Even lying on the sofa wasn't sufficient for me as I would get light-headed and feel like I was going to pass out.

I went from being totally horizontal on my bed for a short while after eating in order to start digesting the food and have enough energy to sit upright.

Recalling how far I had come since then when I was struggling during the long runs, helped boost my confidence so that I could indeed 'do it' and then complete the marathon distance. Each subsequent race I did helped improve my confidence levels as well.

I also reminded myself of the incredible journey I had travelled from leaving Ottawa in 1996 and coming to the UK with no job, no place to live and not knowing anyone. I reminded myself how brave and courageous that was, all because I wanted to 'live the dream' of living and working in the UK, and travel around Europe.

Recalling that experience told me that I must have had a certain amount of confidence in myself and my ability to deal with challenges, even if I did not feel like it at the time! So, if I could do all that, I could do anything!

Those feelings of accomplishment and sense of power in myself gave me the boost I needed to carry on, and do what I needed to do to train for the marathon.

CONFIDENCE

Internal Dialogue

We all have internal chatter that talks to us; whether we actually pay attention to it or whether we are actually aware of it is another thing. Sometimes that internal chatter is positive and logical and other times it is critical, negative and illogical. The positive internal dialogue helps us and supports us to perform well, whereas the negative internal dialogue can actually weaken our performance abilities regardless of the performance arena. Consider a critical parent or coach versus a cheerleader. *Which one helps you to perform better?* We can develop the skills and the habits to turn the volume down on the negative critic and turn up the volume on the cheerleader.

Many of us may not have really taken note of what our thoughts are and how they might affect our performance, yet we all have them. You might be saying right now 'Oh no, I don't hear any chatter!' That is exactly the internal voice I am referring to here, you saying something to yourself! We all have thoughts about what is happening around us. *Have you ever met someone you did not like? What sorts of things did you say to yourself about that person? Did you make up some sort of story or have a picture in your mind as to what they are like?* Whether this story or the picture was true, you still make them up and they will influence how you act and react towards this person.

Moving onto a performance arena, your thoughts about yourself, your competitors and your event will influence how you act and react. *How many of you have gone to a game, a race, or even a training session, feeling negative before you even started?* You might have told yourself that you were tired, that you were not really into the training session that day or that you were feeling distracted by what happened at home or at work. *How was that game, that race or that training session? Did it seem harder than usual?* Now, let us look at things from a different angle. Think of a time when you were feeling pumped up and ready to go. *How did things go then? What was the difference in the outcome that day?*

When you were feeling negative it is most likely that you ended up not doing as well as you might have liked. On the day you were feeling pumped up and ready to go, you played well regardless of whom your opponent was or how big the other team was.

Oftentimes, we are unaware of what our internal dialogue is saying to us and therefore unaware of how it is actually affecting our performances. Therefore, by becoming aware of this internal dialogue, this self-talk, you can monitor what is going on and ensure that it is as positive and supportive as it can possibly be.

WORDS AND THEIR EFFECT

To help you get a better sense of how much of an impact this internal dialogue has on your body and therefore your performance, let us try 'the Chair Exercise'.

- Check things out. Start by becoming more aware of your body, as you sit in your chair right now (assuming of course that you are sitting down reading this book!). Is your weight balanced? Are you sitting tall or slouched, and are there any niggles or twinges? Now, stand up and notice how that feels as you stand up. Did you feel you were balanced or favoured one side? Did you stand up easily or did you have to almost haul yourself out of the seat?

o   Return to your seated position.

- Negative critic. Repeat to yourself 'I am tired, weak, listless, exhausted, afraid. I can't do this.' Use any other combination of 'negative' words. Continue to repeat these words to yourself as you stand up again. Notice what happens with your body and how it feels as you stand up while repeating these 'negative' types of words.

o   Sit down again.

- Positive supporter. Repeat to yourself 'I am strong, powerful, confident, energized, awesome, incredible, flowing' or any other combination of 'positive' words. Continue to repeat these words and stand up again. Notice what you happens with your body and how it feels as you stand up while repeating these 'positive' type of words.

o   OK, exercise over. You can sit down again.

Did you notice how different it was to stand up when you were repeating the negative type of words? You may have said you were tired and it was a struggle to stand up. Yet, when you repeated the positive type of words, you might have leapt out of your chair.

The power of the words you say to yourself does indeed have an effect on the body. Although you may not continually repeat negative or positive type words during your big performances, you do have those fleeting thoughts. Those fleeting thoughts will weaken your physical capabilities and your performance abilities. Additionally, by continually repeating positive-type words to yourself during your performance can help you stay strong, powerful and confident.

WHAT'S GOING ON

Put this into the context of your performance, be that in training or in competition. Negative self-talk and irrational beliefs may leave you feeling upset, angry, irritated, sad, depressed or hopeless. Any negative-type of thought like these will negatively influence and impact on your ability to be the best you can be. *How can you be at the top of your game when your thoughts and feelings are on the floor?* When you are about to perform, the nature of the internal chatter will influence your performance and the outcomes you achieve. If the chatter is negative and unsupportive, just like thinking 'weak, tired or I can't do this' will have a detrimental effect on your ability. Whereas, if the chatter is positive and supportive, just like thinking 'strong, confident, powerful' will have a positive effect on your ability.

The key is firstly to become aware of that chatter and then to evaluate it to determine whether this internal dialogue is positive or negative, before choosing to focus only on the positive talk. Once you become aware of the types of things you say to yourself, the next thing is to turn around any negative chatter so it becomes positive self-talk. We do not pay attention very often to what is going on inside our heads and do not listen. Yet, that negative critic is still there and it is still having an impact on our performance abilities.

Oftentimes, our thoughts fly in so quickly that we barely hear them, and then they fly out just as quickly. Therefore, noticing what our thoughts are is the first step towards doing something about it. To help you notice what your thoughts are, stop right now and think about your thinking. *What are you thinking about?* In addition to reading this book, you might also be thinking about what to eat for dinner, the chores you need to do at the weekend or even what projects need to be completed by the end of the month. So often, our thoughts jump from one thing to the next without us even realizing it.

What are your thoughts when it comes to your performances? What do you think happens when your thoughts jump around from one thing to the next? Without monitoring what your thoughts are, they may actually be hindering your performance. Now, take some time to think of your last event or last training session and then write down what you thought about. Maybe you had thoughts of 'this is hard, I am bored, and I cannot do this'. By writing a list of your thoughts, you can spot the negative, unsupportive or unhelpful things you might say to yourself. By repeating this exercise of writing down your thoughts immediately after an event is even more helpful because the thoughts are still relatively fresh in your mind. You might also write down your thoughts after a training session just to see what types of thoughts you think while training.

By seeing the negative-type statements written down, you can then look at them in a more objective manner to determine whether there is any basis or evidence to support the negative statement. Some questions to ask yourself include:

- *Is it true? What information do I have for this thought?*
- *Do I have any doubt the thought is true? How do I react when I believe that thought?*
- *What evidence exists that contradicts this thought?*

95

- *How often does this thought occur and have I been wrong about this thought before?*
- *What advice would I offer to a friend who had this thought?*
- *Who would I be without the thought?*

These questions are adapted from the four questions in The Work by Byron Katie. The questions are simple yet profound to help uncover what is underneath and what is the reality of the thoughts you have. If there is no basis for those negative, irrational or illogical thoughts, then discard them just like a child letting go of a balloon. See the negative thoughts float away and as a result remove any impact on you. You could also turn things around by coming up with positive statements to replace the negative ones. During your performance event when a random negative thought might surface, you will already be armed with something positive to turn things around.

Here are some examples of negative self-talk and some positive comments to replace them.

Negative self-talk	Positive self-talk
There is a competitor who is better / stronger than me.	I am mentally strong and powerful. I will focus on me, and my own efforts.
I missed that shot and am a poor player.	I will make the next shot and I'm doing my best.
I had a bad start so it's all downhill from here.	I know I can come back and get back on track and perform well.
I made a big mistake and I'm useless.	I can focus on what I am doing now and let go of mistakes.

So, what kind of things do you say to yourself before a big performance event? Is it positive and supportive or is it negative and critical? How can you turn them around so they are helpful and supportive? What sorts of positive things can you say to yourself instead? Write down all these thoughts and then ask the questions to uncover the truth behind them or to dispel them.

What is important when dealing with internal dialogue is to recognize that it is happening and then discard it because it is unfounded or transform it into something more positive and supportive. Yet, much like any habit or new skill that you are developing, you need to pay attention. You need to be consciously aware of that aspect and consciously take action to turn things around or to choose to focus your attention on something else that is more supportive and beneficial to you.

DEALING WITH THE CHATTER

Be aware that your internal dialogue, your self-talk, happens on a continual basis whether you are consciously aware of it or not. This self-talk does have an impact on your performance abilities so ideally you want the dialogue to be positive, supportive and helpful for you to be the best you can be. *When you think back to your past performances, recall your thoughts when you were performing at your best. What were your thoughts when you were performing at your worst?* Again, make sure you write down these thoughts so you can keep track of them and start to notice any patterns that may be emerging after several performances.

When you were performing well, quite probably, your attention was on positive things such as the different tactical elements that help you to perform. A golfer might have focused on their swing, a footballer might focus on driving aggressively towards the net or a triathlete might be feeling the sense of power with each pedal rotation on the bike.

On the other hand, when you were performing poorly, quite possibly, you were focusing on the negatives, the errors or the outcomes. The runner might be worried about the competitor who just passed them, the tennis player about the point they just lost and how much they need to win or the swimmer on the poor start they made.

By noticing the kinds of things you focus on and think about during good and poor performances, you might see a trend. Ideally, you focus on the process of achieving the goal rather than the outcome of actually achieving it. This helps to maintain your attention on what you need to do to be at your best.

Yet, being human, we still have some negative chatter that goes on so here are some tips for dealing with the negative internal dialogue.

- Become aware. Starting paying attention to what you are saying to yourself. Notice whether it is positive and supportive or whether it is negative and critical. *What trends are you noticing and where?*
- Stop sign. Imagine that you have a stop sign flash up, right in front of your face as soon as you notice you have any negative, unhelpful thoughts. This might help jolt you into shifting your thinking to something more positive.
- Ask for proof. Ask yourself whether the chatter actually has any basis of proof in

saying the things it is saying. *Is there any evidence to confirm it is a true statement?* If no proof, then let it go.

- If the chatter is because of pain or discomfort, and you decide that it does not require medical assistance and that you can indeed carry on, then distract yourself with something mundane like counting or singing.

- Positive affirmations. Have a mental 'recording' that continually feeds you positive, supportive, comments such as 'I can do this', 'I am strong, powerful and invincible', and 'I am being the best I can be in each any every moment'. Almost like a mantra that you repeat over and over again to ensure you have positive messages being fed into your brain. Using 'I am …' and 'I can …' statements reinforce the positive messages that you can indeed do what you are doing.

- Play Games. Distract yourself from the negative thoughts with silly childlike games such as focusing on the next lamp post if you are running and draw yourself towards it. Imagine springs on your legs or that your arm is like a catapult for your tennis serve.

There is no right or wrong way to approach this monitoring and changing the internal dialogue. Whatever approach works for you, use it. The key is to become aware of what is going on and asking yourself whether it helps and supports you to perform effectively, or is pulling you down. If it is pulling you down, let it go. Just like any new habit you develop, it takes some time and practice, yet you can get there in the end!

SUMMARY

We all have some sort of internal dialogue going on, and this dialogue does impact on our performance abilities. Sometimes the chatter says negative and critical things to you that may raise doubts, fears, and uncertainty in your ability to perform on the day. This in turn negatively influences your abilities.

By taking time to pay attention to the kinds of things that you say to yourself can help you to ensure that in times of need, you can make sure it is positive and supportive. By taking an objective look at all the things you say to yourself, you can either discard them if there is no basis of truth or turn them around into something positive.

You can be ready with a list of positive, supportive, statements you can repeat to yourself before and during a big event to help boost yourself and be the best you can be. Yet, like any new habit, it takes some attention and some practice so it then becomes easier to spot when the internal dialogue, that self-talk, is unhelpful and then do something about it.

It would be lovely if we never, ever, had any negative internal dialogue. However, more likely than not, you will experience some negative chatter from time to time. Remember, it is a habit and it takes practice before it becomes natural to turn down the volume of the negative chatter and turn up the volume to the positive words of encouragement.

STEPS SUMMARY

1. Develop awareness of what you say to yourself and pay attention to when you say it.

2. Evaluate whether the comments help or hinder your ability to perform.

3. Turn down the volume on the negative, unsupportive type of comments and dismiss the thoughts as soon as they enter your head.

4. Turn up the volume on the positive and supportive ones, and listen to these thoughts more.

5. Have a list of positive affirmative statements that you can use.

MY JOURNEY

My negative internal dialogue was going a mile a minute! I never truly believed I could do what I was embarking upon and that is to run a marathon. Yet, my good friend Lloyd was literally being my personal positive cheerleader!

Any time I uttered a negative thought, he would challenge me in a supportive and friendly way. He helped me to actually see that all the negative things I would say were not based on any evidence. There was no truth in all those things so why not simply let them go!

Lloyd helped me realize that all the negative things I was saying to myself were having a very real and very literal effect on me. When I said that something was too hard, I would actually feel weaker, whereas when I would say at least I would give something a try, that empowered me and helped me to feel stronger.

I particularly experienced this effect as I struggled up big hills and I kept on saying that it was tough. Although hills never became easy, they did become easier when I powered up them repeating positive affirmations to myself and imagined myself springing up the hills as if on giant springs for legs.

Lloyd also helped me to understand that although the negative voice would never totally disappear, I could control how I dealt with it. The idea of turning down the volume much like turning down the volume on unpleasant music on the radio, appealed to me because I did love my music! From there, turning up the volume to the positive things like affirmations I could say to myself, appealed to my ear. There were indeed times that I actually listened to positive and uplifting music just to drown out any of the negative thoughts that kept popping up!

Mental Rehearsal

Most athletes want to be as prepared as possible for their events in terms of performing at their best. They ensure their training has gone according to plan; they have everything they need and they are simply ready to go. All this preparation definitely helps to reassure them that they are ready and when they feel reassured, they undoubtedly perform better. It is those times when they do not feel prepared for their event that increases their sense of stress, anxiety and tension, and as a result, impacts on their performance.

Part of this preparation is doing mental rehearsal. Much like actors rehearse a play before the actual performance, athletes can rehearse their performances as well. For athletes, this rehearsal does not have to be a real performance; it can simply be an imagined one because the brain does not know the difference between what is real and what is imagined. Of course, you still need to train and prepare physically for your event! Yet, mental rehearsal will help you in addition to your physical rehearsal! According to Porter (2003), how you view yourself – your abilities, your acceptability, your intelligence, and your worth – ultimately determines who you become, what you do, and what you have. In other words, you become your reality. Therefore, if you can view yourself and mentally rehearse in the best possible light and achieving your best potential, you are helping to make that a reality.

Mental rehearsal is also referred to as visualisation whereby you see yourself doing what you are about

103

to do. Grout and Perrin (2004, p.153) say "to make the visualization as powerful as possible, you should be seeing the experience through your own eyes – rather than watching yourself as if on a screen. You should also engage all your senses". The more powerful you can imagine a situation, the more likely you will feel as if it were real. So, when you get to the actual event, your brain will think that it has already 'been there, done that'.

BENEFITS OF MENTAL REHEARSAL

Mental rehearsal provides you with the opportunity to explore how you want things to flow and to develop strategies for dealing with unexpected events. It will give you an extra edge when you get to that start line because your brain will believe that it has already done the performance so it knows what to do when you actually get there!

Whatever arena in which you wish to perform, preparation will make a difference to the results and outcomes you achieve. Mental rehearsal also provides you with the opportunity to go through possibilities of what might happen and deal with unexpected situations. Ideally, you want to rehearse best-case scenarios yet equally important is to rehearse how you might handle other scenarios that are not your 'best-case'.

By practicing different scenarios in your mind, you are actually pre-programming yourself to effectively handle and manage whatever comes up on the day. Oftentimes, people say 'expect the unexpected.' Therefore, if something does happen that is not in your best-case scenario plan, you will have more ideas on how you deal with the situation. At least having some ideas that you can call upon will help you devise solutions on the spot.

Otherwise, you may need to make up something as you go along. Having to make up something will take more time and energy versus less energy had you thought beforehand about how you would deal with things.

For example, triathletes and cyclists often worry about what they will do if they get a tyre puncture in a race. By mentally rehearsing dealing with the puncture and easily changing the tyre, they will feel more confident if it were to happen. A golfer might play out in their mind how they would deal with shots that are in the rough or in a bunker. They might even play out how they could get their focus back on track when they are behind.

Mental rehearsal can also give you peace of mind that you know how you will handle anything that comes your way and that you will be able to deal with it. This in turn actually reduces those performance nerves because you are reassured that you will handle any of the unexpected things easily and effortlessly. It can also provide you with the opportunity to strengthen your skill in focusing your attention, dealing with distractions and pouring all your energy into your performance.

REAL OR IMAGINED?

Many sceptics might think that simply imagining your performance will not make a difference to the results you achieve. Yet, so many studies have disproved that! Your brain does not differentiate between what is real and what is imagined. By imagining your best ever performance repeatedly before your actual event, your brain will think it has already done it. Then, on the day of your big event, your brain will think 'been here, done it!' and play out just as you have rehearsed before.

Just to demonstrate how powerful your mind is and how powerful imagined thoughts are, play with a quick exercise to fire up all your senses and see how just thinking some thoughts will affect you. Take a moment to imagine yourself holding a large, juicy lemon in the palm of your hand. See the bright yellow skin and notice the shape and size. Give it a little squeeze and notice how it springs back to your touch. Get a sense of how this fresh, crisp juicy lemon smells. Imagine you are now cutting into the lemon and cut it in half. Notice how the lemon segments looks, how fine the sheath is separating the segments and how strong the smell is of this fresh, juicy lemon. Feel this imaginary lemon in your hand as vividly and richly as possible, seeing the juice and smelling the strong clean scent.

Now, take a bite of this fresh, juicy lemon and feel the juices roll around your mouth.

How was that for you?

For most people, they react in some way to the thought of actually taking a bite of a lemon. Their mouth waters and even puckers as if they were actually, really, biting into that lemon. *Did yours?* You may have reacted to biting into this imaginary lemon, even though you did not bite into a real one. Your brain was giving you a very real and very physical reaction to something you have simply imagined!

Need more convincing? Let's look at another scenario: *Have you ever woken up in the middle of the night after hearing a sound and your heart was racing?* You were not sure quite sure why you woke up, yet you knew you were fearful of something. Perhaps every fibre in your body was awake, alert and ready to jump. More often than not, there is no real threat or danger – it was simply a dream. Even though it was a dream, you still physically reacted as if it were real.

These two examples illustrate that the mind does not differentiate between real and imagined events. It simply reacts to the thoughts you have and how you have interpreted those thoughts. So, how does this relate to sports performances? You are aware how you can physically react to imagined situations such as holding a lemon, therefore, you can also physically react to your imagined sporting events.

By imagining your performance event in as much detail as possible and getting a sense of the actual feelings you will feel on the day, both physically and mentally, will help you 'react' when you get to the actual event. The added bonus by doing this mental rehearsal is that you will have more energy for your actual performance on the day because you are aware of all the things you have to do.

How many of you have run around on the day of a big event, feeling nervous, and worried that you would forget something or that something would go wrong? All this running around and worrying uses up energy that could be much better used for other things – such as your performance! This concept of energy in your body is similar to fuel in a car or your personal rechargeable batteries. The fuel in the car is used to drive the car forward. The energy in your body is used to help you perform. If you expend energy running around before your event, you will then have less to pour into your performance.

So, let's look at how conserving energy is related to mental rehearsal. Quite simply, one way to reduce the nervous energy expenditure is to rehearse. When you know what to expect and what to do, the prospect of actually performing seems less stressful. When you know what to do and when you need to do it, you will feel calmer and therefore expend less nervous energy beforehand.

WHAT TO REHEARSE

You may be wondering what specifically you should be rehearsing. Well, you can mentally rehearse your entire event from start to finish! You can mentally rehearse the day of your event or even rehearse how you will orchestrate your activities and actions days before the event. To sum up what you can rehearse, it is everything and anything! The important thing is to not just 'see' what steps and actions you will take yet also get a sense of how you will 'feel' when you are taking these steps.

Make sure to include everything and everyone you might come into contact with. Include some contingency plans for dealing with the unexpected. I know unexpected events are exactly that – unexpected. However, if you can rehearse some typical scenarios of the 'what ifs', this will indeed help you on the day because at least you will have some idea of how to deal with them. I am by no means suggesting you focus on the negatives during your mental rehearsal. Focus on you being at your best.

Yet, by exploring some of the potential negative scenarios, you will likely feel better prepared to deal with them should they occur! In the event something happens that you had not rehearsed, you will at least have some resources for dealing with other scenarios and will be able to draw from these to help you manage the situation.

Make sure you include such things as what you are going to eat for breakfast in the morning, how you are going to travel to the event, what you will be wearing and how you will warm up. You might mentally rehearse your specific warm-up routine and even moments before the start of the event. Perhaps you are in the changing room with your teammates, or in a holding area with other competitors, so pay attention to how will you be acting and where will your focus be.

Then, as the gun goes off and the race is on, get a sense of how you feel being strong, confident and powerful. Get a sense of how you feel as the race progresses with all your thoughts and all your energy directed towards you doing what you need to do. Make sure you also include how you feel after you have completed your event, how amazing it feels to have given it your best shot knowing that you could not have done any more on the day.

Overall, what is important here when you mentally rehearse your performance is to not just 'see' what you will see, and also 'experience' it all. Imagine what you will hear and imagine how you will feel. You could even add tastes and smells. The richer and more vibrant you can experience this rehearsal, the better it will be for you! Add as much detail as you can possibly think of so you are helping to create this reality.

SUMMARY

To be the best you can be, you would not dream about going into a game cold or running a race without warming up or even not knowing your opponent. Doing some mental preparation is the same as physically warming up before your event. This ultimately helps you be the best you can be on the day.

Mentally rehearsing, or visualising how you will perform on the day, helps to plant the seeds in the brain so it knows what to do on the day. Although you want to visualise best-case scenarios, you will also benefit from rehearsing the 'what-ifs' situations to give you more confidence and ideas to deal with the unexpected, if they were to happen!

It is the same as practicing a technical skill such as hitting a tennis ball or kicking a football. These practical skills require repeated practice until they become effortless and can be done without any conscious thought. By mentally visualising your performance, you will then be able to execute that particular skill effortlessly and without conscious thought on the day. Your brain will think 'Hey I've been here before and I know what to do!' and will do it!

STEPS SUMMARY

1. Imagine your performance from start to finish, as best-case scenario and include how you will feel.

2. Add in the 'what ifs' scenarios and experience yourself handling things easily and effortlessly.

3. Repeat visualisation regularly, ideally on a daily basis, and prior to your big event.

MY JOURNEY

I never did really believe that simply by imagining my run, or my race, could make a difference. I did not appreciate how powerful the mind is until a fellow runner talked about taking a bite out of a lemon. Just thinking about biting into a lemon did nothing for me. However, by imagining in great detail what it would look like, feel like, smell like and then taste like … my mouth watered! I was reacting to something I had only imagined! This little exercise helped me to understand the strength of the mind and what effect it can have on the body. Much like listening to a great song or piece of music, looking at old photographs that bring back happy memories, those feel good feelings come back again. I wanted to tap into those feel good feelings for my long runs and my races. So, I practiced the race in my mind!

While I was training for my marathon, I did some visualisation exercises before each long run. I would even imagine myself at times being negative yet being able to catch myself and turn the thoughts around so that I complete the run with ease, and with a smile on my face at the end. OK, so sometimes it was a silly grin of fatigue and exhaustion however I was still smiling!

I soon realized that there was a difference between the runs where I did some mental rehearsal beforehand and those times when I did not. Perhaps it was all in my mind, yet I certainly felt a positive difference when I actually did them, the runs actually felt easier. Plus, when I went to races, the mental rehearsal certainly helped to calm me because I knew what I had to do. I knew I had a plan and it was simply a question of executing that plan.

Event Performance

This next section, Event Performance, aims to introduce you to the skills, strategies and techniques that you can use on the day of your event to help you be the best you can be. These additional strategies need to be practiced before your event so that you can use them effortlessly on the day of your event.

One of the key skills is **relaxation**. The ability to relax is critical to an athlete's ability to perform effectively. Being able to instantly and effortlessly relax, with simply one breath, is a skill that with practice comes easily and can help you in many different situations. To a certain degree, some nervous tension can excite you and fire you up for the performance. However, when the balance tips towards the 'negative' side of stress, it hinders your ability to perform effectively. Developing the ability to instantly relax will help you with your performances and all your interactions when you feel any tension rising.

Routines are another element of achieving peak performance. Many of us get up each day and go about life almost on autopilot. This is particularly true about getting up and out of the house to work each day! We do not have to think too much about what we are doing, we simply do what is necessary to arrive at work on time where we then switch our brains on to function at work. When you have a performance event, your preparation and routine should be as familiar to you as getting up each day. You switch to autopilot and do not have to feel stressed about what to do; you simply do it. This reduces your sense of stress and contributes to you getting into what athletes call 'the zone'. Your pre-event routine will be personal to you and may even contain a checklist of things to do and what to pack for the event. Through practice, you can make any adjustments of what worked well and what did not work so well so that you fine-tune your routine to suit your individual needs.

The next skill in this event performance area is all about improving your **focus**. It is important to pay attention only to those things that positively contribute towards your performance and to disregard those things that detract from your performance. During your preparation, it is important that you maintain focus on what you need to do to prepare and train for your big event. For the actual performance day, you need to have identified what helps and what hinders your performance, and pay attention only to those things that help you.

Having mastered these skills, all that there is left to do is simply perform. Allow your body to do what you have trained it to do knowing that you have also trained your mind to help you.

Relaxation

Many of us go about life each day, running from one place to the next without even noticing what is going on in our bodies. We simply rely on the fact that the body will support us in all that we want to do. Rarely do we actually stop to notice how much tension and stress is held in the body. It is only when this stress and tension reaches such a degree of intensity that we have no choice and we have to take notice.

When you want to perform for a big event, and your adrenaline levels are high, there is generally an increase in stress and tension. It is therefore important to recognize the fine balance between good, positive stress that fuels you up and sharpens your focus and negative, detrimental stress, that inhibits your performance abilities. In order to be able to perform to the best of your abilities, you need to be aware of this delicate balance to ensure that you stay on the positive side of stress to fuel your performance. It is in this positive state that you are more easily in the flow of things and your body can do what you have trained it to do.

Unfortunately, many performers get so nervous before a big event that their nerves detract from this ability to be the best they can be. So, for them, being able to relax, calm those nerves, and use the adrenaline energy that is coursing through their bodies to fuel their performances, rather than detract from it, will make a big difference.

Breathing is an essential part of the relaxation process and it is important to recognize how much your

115

breathing does indeed affect how well you perform. Many of us do not pay any attention whatsoever to our breathing. It is usually when we are working out hard that we notice how laboured our breathing may have become! By developing an awareness of our breathing when we are not working hard, you can then develop the skill to use it to relax you in one conscious breath. Before we move on to developing the skill of instant relaxation in one conscious breath, let us look at what happens in the body when stress increases.

According to Dahlkoetter (2003), relaxation does for the mind what stretching does for the body. Even though it may be counter-intuitive to think about relaxing the body before you need to be ready to perform, relaxation does have a beneficial effect on both the body and mind. Athletes do need a certain amount of tension to perform well, yet when there is too much tension, their performance actually decreases. Additionally, with too much tension, they do not think as clearly or quickly as when they are more relaxed.

To help you relax, the first step is to identify those things that stress you.

WHAT ARE YOUR STRESSORS?

A good first step towards reducing that sense of stress, anxiety, and even panic before your big event is knowing exactly what people, places, and things cause you to experience that stress in the first instance. Every time these distractions appear, they have a negative impact on your focus and your abilities. Yet, by knowing in advance what sorts of things bother you, you can put in place strategies to minimize either their occurrence or how you react to them.

Start by listing the people, places, or things that lead up to and during your performances that unnerve you, rattle your cage and distract you from the task at hand. This might sound familiar to looking at the people, places and things that drain you and that fuel you. Now, we are looking specifically at your performance environment to see what may be having an impact or influence on you. For some athletes, just knowing another competitor is turning up on the day unsettles them. Sometimes, it is getting off to a bad start at the beginning of the race, for example when a triathlete gets punched in the swim or loses their goggles. Perhaps it is even a coach, parent or friend saying something that unnerves an athlete and sends them into a wobble about their ability to do what they are about to do.

One of the biggest stressors for many athletes is themselves and their expectations for their performance. These expectations are self-imposed goals and beliefs about how they will perform. Yet sometimes these expectations are not realistic and are outside of their control. It is therefore critical to recognize your own expectations for performing as part of the things that m a y negatively stress you and negatively impact on your performance.

By writing down all the things that stress you and negatively impact o n your performance, you can then look at them more objectively and determine what things you can control and what strategies you can put in place to minimize their negative effect. For example, if being around certain individuals increases your sense of stress, then simply avoid them or minimize contact with them. If being around all the other competitors before the race unnerves you, find a quiet place to be by yourself and focus on what you need to do for you. Do something to make you feel good about you, and remember, assess your expectations for your performance to ensure they are realistic and within your control.

For those things you cannot control, such as being in a holding pen before heading out for your race, have strategies and ideas for how you will deal with them resourcefully and positively so the negative impact is minimized. For example, some swimmers will listen to music and imagine they are in their own little bubble where other competitors are on the outside. Another thought is to remind yourself of everything you can do to be at your best so that you focus on yourself rather than what or who is around you.

Having strategies in place for stressful situations will help you to perform at your best. Yet, athletes often still become stressed, which in turn negatively impacts on their performance abilities.

INCREASE IN STRESS, DECREASE IN PERFORMANCE

How many of you can relate to when you are just about to start your race or undertake a challenge and are feeling somewhat nervous and stressed? You may be doing something you have never done before or wonder whether you have prepared enough. As the nervous mental stress rises, so does the tension in the physical body. The net result is that you are less able to physically perform than if you were relaxed.

Butler and Hope (1995) have an excellent analogy for getting the balance just right. They describe the pressure of a car tyre. If the pressure is just right, you have a smooth ride. If the pressure is too low, you feel all the bumps in the road, whereas if the pressure is too high, you bounce around and easily swing out of control. From a performance perspective, there is equally a fine balance.

Figure 2 shows the effects of stress on performance.

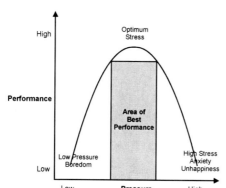

Figure 2 : Performance and Pressure Relationship

This figure illustrates how your performance is affected if you do not have enough stress or if you have too much stress. There must be an ideal balance for an ideal performance. Oftentimes in a performance situation, the pre-race nerves and perceived negative stress means that muscles become tighter, breathing becomes shallower and more rapid and the heart rate increases. As you become tighter and tense, your physical body is not as fluid (which is essential in any physical activity) and your mind may not think as clearly (which is essential in any mental activity). When you become stressed, from a mental perspective, you may even experience doubts, worry or fear, and may feel a sense of frustration, confusion or even panic.

It is therefore important to develop an awareness of stress and where tension is held in the body in order to then develop the skill to help you release that tension and relax. This in turn will contribute towards you performing even better. On a physical level, when you relax, your body instantly becomes more fluid and moves

119

with less effort. From a mental perspective, you will be able to think more clearly, logically and rationally. Plus, you will also use up less of your internal energy and therefore have more available to pour into your performance.

To help you recognize what stress and tension feel like in the body, here is an exercise to develop your awareness. Wherever you are now, do an 'internal body check'. Firstly, notice how you are sitting. *How comfortable are you feeling? Are you feeling balanced and square or tilted from one side to another? How do your shoulders feel? Are they relaxed or somewhat tense? How is your breathing? Deep or shallow? Do you feel some tension or do you feel calm and relaxed?* Bring your attention now to around your eyes and imagine letting go of all the tension there. *Did you notice any shift?* This internal body check is simply to help you take notice of what is going on within you.

Taking time to do an internal body check at different times just helps you to develop an awareness of your physical body and where you might be holding any tension. Often we are unaware that in fact we are holding some tension, even when we do not feel particularly stressed. In turn, this awareness can help us then release any tension when we are about to perform.

So, let us look at several exercises that can help you to get more relaxed.

PROGRESSIVE MUSCLE RELAXATION

This technique is to help you progressively and very consciously relax all your muscles. This in turn will help calm those nerves and help improve your performance. The first step as you start this exercise is to take a moment to notice whether you are holding any tension. As we have just previously motioned above, take a few moments to notice what is going on inside your body. *Do you notice any tension in your body? How about your shoulder area, your face or even around the eyes?*

To illustrate the effect that tight, tense muscles have on you, much like when we are holding stress, take a moment to tense all your muscles. Contract all the muscles in your legs, your arms, your abdomen, even your shoulders and face. Now, try doing the movements you do in your sport. *How easy is it for you to move when you are tight and tense like this?* Relax all your muscles now and do the movements again. *How different is it for you to move when you are tense and tight, and when you are relaxed?* Most likely, when you are tense and tight, the movements are difficult whereas when you are relaxed, the movements are easier.

Just before your competition, you might not be as tense and tight as you have just tried to be; however, the principle is the same. The more relaxed you can feel and move, the easier the movements will be. Following on, the easier the movements are, the more effective you will perform and in turn, help you to be at your best.

To do this progressive muscle relaxation exercise, start with simply bringing your attention to your breath and notice your chest and abdomen rise with each in breath. When you exhale, notice your chest fall.

Now bring your attention to your feet. Contract the muscles in your feel, hold for five seconds and then release. Slowly move your attention to your calves, contract the muscles, hold for five seconds and then release.

Continue to progress up the body and focus on one area at a time from the thighs, the abdomen, the chest, the arms, the neck and shoulders, the face and then the eyes.

As you contract and release each big muscle group, notice the difference in how you feel. Notice the difference between how you feel when the muscles are contracted and when they are relaxed. With practice, you can do a quick scan of the body to sense where you might be holding any tension, and then release it. So, if you notice any tension just before you are about to go on and do your event, imagine contracting and tightening that area up just like you did during the progressive muscle relaxation exercise, and release it.

ONE CONSCIOUS BREATH

Coupled with the progressive muscle relaxation exercise is doing some deep breathing exercises. Taking one deep breath is very effective in helping to relax before your event. This one conscious deep breath helps to calm your nerves and relax the body. It may be referred to by many names including deep abdominal breathing or belly breathing, yet what this breath does is give a signal to the body that all is well and calms that 'fight or flight' response. Think about it, if you are feeling calm about something, that automatic response to stress is not triggered. By taking a slow, deep breath, you are effectively telling the body that everything is OK and there is no need to fight or take flight to survive.

To practise this deep breathing, take a breath in through your nose and out through your nose. When you breathe in, imagine the air filling up your abdomen (not your chest) and let the air expand your abdomen naturally. Hold your breath for about five seconds, and then slowly exhale. To make this deep breathing exercise even more effective, imagine that with each out breath, you are releasing all the tension from the body. Get a real sense of how this feels in the body as you experience the muscles actually releasing. You only have to do this conscious relaxing breathing for about 5–10 breaths to have a noticeable effect on how you feel.

Practising deep abdominal breathing during training means that you will be able to easily call upon this relaxed state in a demanding situation, such as before a competition or just before you take a shot. With practice, you can progress to simply taking one conscious breath to feel instantly relaxed.

When you are feeling relaxed, you will be able to perform more effectively. A good way to practise the one conscious breath is following the progressive muscle relaxation exercise because you will already be in a calm state. This is along the same lines as the confidence anchor where you created a link between a trigger and a response. So, you create an anchor with the trigger of one conscious breath and the response is a sense of relaxation and calm. The great thing about using one conscious breath as an anchor for relaxation and calmness is that no one knows what you are doing because you are simply doing what we all do – and that is to breathe.

Ideally, at every practice session, take the time to develop your awareness of where any tension is being held in the body and develop the skill to relax. This practice will help you when it comes to your actual performance event when the adrenalin is high and you are about to perform. Since you have practised relaxing during times when the stress levels might not have been as high, you will know how effective it can be and what a difference it will make.

GROUNDING AND CALMING

Another means to help relax you before a competition is by 'grounding' yourself. The idea of grounding is common practice within the martial arts disciplines and is a good preparation to help be mentally focused and physically prepared. In other sports arenas, grounding can help with calming the nerves. Much like a tennis player waiting to receive their opponents' shot or a martial artist ready for a fight, they are very grounded and strong in how they stand, ready to move in any direction necessary.

To start developing your skill of grounding yourself, you would simply stand up, whereas the more advanced manner is to stand in the position when you are about to perform your activity such as when you are just about to hit that tennis ball, kick the football or run down the field. To help you develop an awareness of being grounded, try the following:

- **Stand up in an upright and balanced manner.** Stand up with your weight evenly distributed between your feet and arms hanging loosely by your side. Just stand there and bring your attention to your breathing in a relaxed manner.
- **Imagine a horizontal line and a vertical line in your body.** Imagine that you have a horizontal line dividing your body in half. Now imagine you have a vertical line dividing your body in half. Where the horizontal and vertical lines meet is your centre point. Generally, these lines intersect in the middle of your body slightly behind and below your navel.

- **Shift your centre point**. Play around with moving the horizontal line higher and lower which shifts your centre point higher and lower. Now, play with shifting the vertical line to the left and then to the right. When you play around with shifting your centre point, you might notice different sensations in the body. For some people, shifting the centre point lower might give them a heavier sensation in the legs whereas higher might give them a lighter feeling.

Within a sporting context, becoming grounded has a calming effect and gives you sense of being more solid and stronger. Then, when in play, some athletes might have lower or higher centre points depending on their sport. A tennis player might have a higher centre point before they serve the ball, as they want to have more weight and hence power in their upper body for their serve. A golfer might have a centre point a bit lower while addressing the ball and then shift it higher than middle when swinging the club.

The important thing in grounding is to play around and see what works best for you. *Do you need to shift the centre point during your event and in what situation do you need to shift it?* Perhaps you could practise different body placements that you might be in during your event from standing, running, hitting, gesturing, etc.

SUMMARY

We all experience a certain amount of stress in our lives, and this stress is usually increased when we have a big event where we want to perform at our best. Yet, when the stress becomes too much and becomes more negative, it detracts from our performance abilities. When we allow ourselves to become almost overwhelmed with stress, we are effectively holding ourselves back and inhibiting our ability to flow naturally, effortlessly and easily.

Recognizing what your body feels like when you experience stress and tension then helps you to direct your attention to releasing it. By practising progressive muscle tension and relaxation helps you to experience the differences between tense and tight muscles, and relaxed muscles. Using an out-breath with visualization to release any tension can help even further to achieve that relaxed state. You can use this increased awareness of how your body feels holding tension and how it feels when it is relaxed to help feel calmer before any big event.

Developing the skill of instant relaxation can help you in most situations in your life where ideally you want to be relaxed, fluid and at ease. Instant relaxation can come about simply through the awareness of tension in a particular muscle and then releasing it mentally or through the use of an anchor like one conscious breath. In addition, by practising being grounded, not only does it help you feel calmer, it also helps you feel stronger when you perform. You can use this for a particular movement in your sport or simply when having a difficult discussion with someone.

Reminding yourself that you do indeed perform better when you are relaxed is a good incentive to master this particular mental skill. Plus, it can help you in many other 'stressful' situations that you encounter in life.

STEPS SUMMARY

1. Do an internal body check to notice where any tension is being held in your body.

2. Do some Progressive Muscle Relaxation exercises to relax your body from your feet all the way up to your head, including around the eyes.

3. Consciously use an out-breath to imagine any tension leaving a specific part of your body or your whole body.

4. Practise using the One Conscious Breath anchor in any situation in life where you want to achieve relaxation in an instant.

5. Play around with grounding to help relax you, help you feel more solid and stronger, and when you are performing your sport.

MY JOURNEY

I was never that relaxed before any race (I was more like a bag of nerves!) and the thought of doing relaxation exercises before a race was the furthest thing from my mind.

I did however see a difference in my energy levels! I was very tuned into my energy levels and knew that if I did get stressed, I would quickly lose energy. Therefore, I appreciated that doing what I could to relax before a race would help me to get through the race.

With the incentive of simply being able to complete the race distance, I did what I could to calm those nerves. The progressive muscle relaxation was usually done before I left home in the quiet of my own space. It was also easier because I had fewer distractions around me. The One Conscious Breath was

127

very easy to do, as was the 'grounding' when I got to the start line. These helped me to feel calmer and even stronger within myself. Sometimes I would take several 'one conscious breaths' to calm myself down and help me feel less affected by those pre-race nerves. I also liked the fact that these relaxing techniques helped me elsewhere in life because I often found myself tense, tight and feeling stressed in challenging situations.

The ability to easily and quickly release any tension in my body, feel calm in an instant with one breath or even feel stronger within myself was like magic for me. No one knew what I was doing because it was all going on inside my head, yet it made a big positive difference to how I felt.

Routines

Take a moment to think about your morning routine of getting up and out the door for the day. For most of us, it does not take much thought or energy. You are simply on autopilot and do what you need to do. The only thinking might be what to wear on the day or what to eat for breakfast. Otherwise, it is pretty simple and straightforward. *Right?*

Now, think of a time when you had to get up earlier than usual, for example, an early morning appointment or going away on holiday and needed to get to the airport at an early hour. *How did you sleep the night before? What was the difference in getting up and out the door compared to your regular day-to-day routine? Were you on autopilot or worried about things?* For most of us, this disruption in our routine meant we did not sleep as well the night before and our stress levels were just a bit higher before we got out the door.

When our daily routines are disrupted, we have to think more about what to do and when to do it, simply because it is new or different from our familiar pattern. This additional thought can cause some of us to feel more stressed. Applying this concept of routine to a big performance event such as a race, the more familiar we are with our routine, the more we will go on autopilot and simply do what we need to do. This familiarity will help keep the stress levels lower and in turn, help improve performances.

Although you may not have big performance events every day, you can develop routines for your training sessions and practise them at smaller events before you put them into play for bigger, more important, events.

ROUTINES AND PERFORMANCE

From a performance perspective, you can benefit from developing a 'pre-event routine' and even have checklists of everything you need so that when it comes to the actual event, you do not have to think – you simply do. You can look at your written list of everything you do and simply 'tick them off' as you do them. Lynch and Scott (1999) found that the more familiar with your pre-event routine, the more you have control over anxiety. Routines, or rituals as they are also referred to, are habits that require little or no thought and this in turn is relaxing, reduces tension and reduces fear about forgetting something.

Loehr and Schwartz (2003) also talk about rituals from an energy perspective in order to minimize unnecessary energy expenditure, thereby having more energy for your performances. Loehr and Schwartz (2003, p. 173) say "rituals provide a source of security and consistency without thwarting change or undermining flexibility".

Yet, because we are all creatures of habit, some of what we do helps us and contributes towards us being the best we can be while other habits may make us even more nervous and detract from our performances. For example, a good habit might include preparing all the clothing, the equipment and the food on the day before a race while a poor habit might be always to arrive at the last minute to the race venue and rush to the start line simply because that is what you always do.

It is important to understand that some routines might be good for you while others are not. The key is to explore carefully the things you do to prepare for your event and identify those actions, habits and thoughts that are beneficial and those that are not. With this insight of what helps and hinders, you can then go on to develop a checklist of your ideal pre-event routine preparation. To help you understand whether a routine is effective for you, you need to ask yourself whether you are expending energy unnecessarily or conserving your energy. Is it helping you or hindering you. Is it calming you or is it making you more nervous and anxious.

Let us explore two scenarios as a way to demonstrate this difference.

In the first scenario, Person A is going to participate in a big running race. On the morning of their event, they are running around their home gathering all what they need for the event and packing their bags. They know they need clothes for the event and for afterwards, they need their shoes, maybe even towels, food, and drinks for pre-event, during the event and post-event. They might be worried that they forget something, e.g. their race number, and have to check a few times just to reassure themselves that they have everything. They might also wonder whether they included their lucky socks. Then, they get lost on their way to the event because they thought they knew where they were going however took a wrong turn. When they finally find the start of the event, they are rushing around getting themselves sorted, do a very brief warm up because they ran out of time for a proper warm up and get to the start line feeling rushed, flustered and maybe even somewhat stressed.

Person B is participating in the same big event and they have packed their bags the night before with everything they know they will need to bring. They have verified where the race starts and how to get there, and know what time they have to get up, what time they need to eat and when to leave for the event. They arrive in sufficient time, even allowing extra time for parking, complete their pre-race warm up in sufficient time and leisurely wait in the queue for the loo before the start of the race.

Comparing the two scenarios, how much energy do you think Person A and Person B will have to focus on their event performance? Person A has expended a lot of energy by rushing around and worrying, and are probably quite mentally distracted. Person B has conserved their energy because they had their pre-event routine in place and did things as they always do them. They are probably quite mentally focused. The difference between these two individuals is that one has a set routine they follow for all their big events and therefore it minimizes the amount of stress they expend on the day. They have conserved energy prior to their performance, and therefore have more energy to direct towards their efforts.

The key to routines is to minimize stress and have a familiar set of actions to complete. You do not have to think about what to do because you are simply following the list of what to do and when to do it. This reduces any nervous energy expenditure and helps you to stay calm, clear-headed and have more energy to pour into your performance efforts.

PAST PERFORMANCES

To help you develop your own personal routine, the first step is to reflect and gather information related to past performances. By examining what you have done in the past, you can start putting together the elements for your next big performance. You can start this process by first recalling some of your past performances – both good and not so good. Write down all the things you did to get yourself ready, prepared and to the start line of your race.

Once you have identified some past performances, look carefully at, and reflect upon, everything you did that contributed towards your performance. In terms of any sporting discipline, you can go into great detail about your actual training and preparation regime. However, what I want you to focus on here is looking at what was happening on the day and the evening before the event and on the day itself. Some things to include are:

- *What sorts of activities did you do? What was the balance between resting and other activities?*
- *What foods did you eat or not eat?*
- *When did you prepare all your clothes and equipment to take to the event? Did you know what to take?*
- *How organized or disorganized were you? What could you have done differently?*
- *What people, places and things were you around? How did they influence or impact on your ability to stay focused?*
- *How did you get to the event and who was responsible for figuring out directions and logistics?*
- *On the morning of the event, when did you eat before the event? What did you eat?*
- *What specifically did you to do warm up and prepare for the event? Who was around you?*

All these questions are meant as prompts to help you think about what you did for different performances.

By drawing up a list of all the things you do that contribute to a good performance, you can then use it again when you want to achieve another good performance! This list might include elements such as your food intake on the day before and the day of the competition, the amount of rest you had or the people that were around you. Some people like the distraction of friends and family around to support them before a race, whereas other competitors like to have the hour before the race to themselves to mentally prepare and get more focused on the task at hand.

Knowing what elements help you to perform at your best, you can then repeat them. Repeat what works well and contributes to good performances and either eliminate or modify those things that detract from your performances. For example, if you know that you perform better when someone else drives you to the event than when you drive yourself, then arrange for someone to drive you when you want to achieve a great performance for a big event! If you know that you need an hour of quiet time by yourself to get 'into the zone' before the start, then even if family and friends have come to support you, make sure you take this quiet time.

Recognize that we are all unique in how we react to situations and what works well for one person might not work well for another. It is therefore beneficial to try out your own personal checklist and pre-event routine for training sessions and less important events so when it comes to a big important event, you know you have a checklist and routine that works for you! Sometimes it is through trial and error of what you need to include in your own checklist. If you get to a race and think 'I should have brought this or that,' be sure to add it to your list for the next time. One triathlete stayed in campsites rather than in hotels before their event if there was a distance greater than one and a half hours to travel. After one experience, they added 'bring own toilet paper … just in case' to their checklist!

DEVELOPING YOUR ROUTINE

Each individual knows best what works well for them and therefore there is no one clear-cut routine or checklist that works for everyone and for all performance events. Lynch and Scott (1999) state that everything you do in the last 48 hours before your race should form part of your ritual routine. All what you do helps to physically and mentally prepare for your race so that when the gun goes off or the match is about to begin, you are as prepared and ready to go as you can be.

There are some basic things that you can consider for similar events. Below are some things you could include in your pre-event routine for any sports-related performance. Try them out and see what you need for your event. Make sure you review the list after each event and make any adjustments for the next time by adding things you forgot or removing things that you do not need.

For top-level performers, their routines might even start a week prior to their big event. For other athletes, they have a routine that starts the day before or perhaps just on the day of the event.

When you initially start using a pre-event routine, I encourage you to write it out and consult it as you prepare for your event. Lynch and Scott (1999) suggests that a checklist could include such things as travel arrangements (car filled up with petrol, driving directions to destination and even how much time it will take you), what time to set the alarm (or two if you want to be extra sure to get up in time!), all the food and clothes you want and need to bring, etc.

135

This pre-event checklist is much like a list of things to bring on a school trip or going away to summer camp. Your checklist acts as a reminder and can help you to do everything and bring everything you need to do for your event. Using checklists is also a way to minimize your energy expenditure prior to your event because you do not have to think about things, you simply do them. The aim of having a checklist is to ensure that everything you need to do or think about is done. Plus, you do not have to worry about missing or forgetting things.

Your personal event checklist might include all things you need to do upon arrival at your event, what materials or equipment you need, even what clothes you want to wear. The checklist might even cover things you want to do from the time you get up in the morning to the time you arrive at your event.

Whatever you think is relevant for your performance; include it in the checklist as you can always ignore that particular item, yet at least it may prompt you to think about it. Whether you actually need it for that particular performance event is another thing. For example, you might include a prompt about cloths for warm weather and cold weather, depending on what the forecast is for the day. Then make the decision what to bring when you actually prepare your kit.

To give you a few suggestions of what might be included in a sports-performance checklist and pre-event routine, here are some ideas. Remember, each individual will need to customize their checklist and routine for their personal needs and their event.

Week prior to event

- Eating – ensure you consume healthy foods that you are used to and that provide quality fuel for your body. *Do you want or need to eat specific types of foods leading up to your event? Do you need to bring this yourself or can you get it where you are staying?*

- Resting – ensure you get sufficient rest, possibly more than normal, before the event. Also, avoid any unnecessary expenditure of energy or activities. *Do you need to get additional rest or sleep before your event? How many hours sleep do you like to get to perform at your best?*
- Exercise – Keep your body moving to maintain flexibility without putting added strain or demands on it. *How do you need to adjust your training schedule and taper before the race? Do you need to do some specific stretching or get a massage?*
- Other activities – *Do you need to reduce additional activities that you do such as walking around visiting a new city before a big event or taking time off work the day before?*
- Self-care – Do whatever makes you feel good about yourself and your life. This might mean taking time out for you before a big event or perhaps surrounding yourself with positive, supportive, friends. *What sorts of activities contribute to your overall sense of well-being? How could you incorporate some of them into your schedule just before the event?*
- Distractions – Minimize the distractions placed on you. This might mean that you have to isolate yourself away from the normal day-to-day demands of life. *What sorts of things do you find distracting and take away from your focus of your performance? What could you put in place to minimize these distractions?*

- Visualisation exercises – Regularly visualise perfect racing form and the perfect race. Include aspects of the course/landmarks, the supporters and entertainment, water stations, when and where to drink and eat. *How vividly can you imagine your performance? What will you see, hear and even experience during the event?*
- Repeat positive self-talk such as 'I have done all the training, I will complete the distance and feel strong and powerful.' *Do you have a written list of positive affirmations that you can review just before you perform?*

Day before event

- Arrange all your clothes, food required for pre-, during, and post-event. Make sure you have a list of all the things that you might need or want to bring with you, and check them off when you pack.
- Confirm travel arrangements and directions.
- Calculate what time to set alarm clock to get up and do the necessary things before leaving the house, e.g. time for breakfast, shower, stretching, etc.
- Get breakfast food prepared beforehand as much as possible. For example, all the food and cutlery you need out on the counter. This will help to speed things up in the morning.
- Remind yourself what you are going to do, the sequence of events, in the morning and when, before leaving the house. This could be similar to a countdown that counts back from when the race starts all the way to when you get up in the morning.

Day of event

- Execute your 'day of event' routine for when to get up before event and everything you need to do to get to the event.
- Warm up physically and mentally by doing a stretching routine in a specific sequence and doing your mental rehearsal.
- Plan for loo stops / comfort breaks to use the washroom facilities.
- Review game plan for event – this is your personal strategy for the event and your goals.
- Review list of positive affirmations, and list of positive statements you can use to turn around any negative dialogue.

During event

- Maintain focus on you, on what you are doing and on your own game plan.
- Do regular assessments to check progress and make any adjustments as required. For example, a runner might check how they are feeling to decide whether their pace can change.
- Maintain the positive self-talk to reassure yourself that you have completed all the necessary training to achieve the goal, and that you are strong and healthy.
- Focus on your performance, your effort and your own race plan, rather than the outcome of the race.

When you have your checklist and implement your pre- event routine, *how do you feel at the start of your event? How are your energy levels just prior to, and during your event? Do you feel as if you are calmer, more focused and ready for action, knowing that you have done all the preparation you need to do?*

A checklist takes the thinking out of your preparation. You simply have to do all that is written down in your pre-event routine. The important thing is to develop a routine that works for you so that you can go on autopilot before an event, much like your routine when you get up and go to work in the morning. Over time, your checklist may evolve. It is therefore a good thing to review the list to see if there are any changes to be made after each event.

SUMMARY

Routines minimize stress and unnecessary energy expenditure before an event. Routines also help to ensure that you do all that you need to do to perform effectively. By developing a set routine, you can operate almost as if on autopilot before any performance event, thereby having more energy available for your event performance and more energy means a stronger performance.

It is important to recognize that routines are unique to each individual. What works for one person might be very different from what works for another person. For some individuals, they start their pre-event routine a week before a big event. They watch what they eat, what they do, and the people they are in contact with. The most critical aspect of a pre-event routine is the day before and the day of the event so that everything proceeds like clockwork.

In order to develop your own pre-event routine, you benefit from writing out the elements to consider for the week prior to the event, the day before the event and the morning of the event. Play around with the various elements to see what works best for you so you have your own individual checklist of what to do and when to do it. Of course, these can be adjusted for each event, yet all the basics are there to consider. Much like getting up and out the door in the morning to get to work, your pre-event routine can help you keep calm and simply do what you need to do without much thought.

STEPS SUMMARY

1. Identify what you did for past events to prepare and distinguish the differences between when you had good performances and disappointing performances.

2. Review what you did and come up with your own 'recipe for success' of what worked well.

3. Develop a checklist of all the resources you might need or want for your event.

4. Write out your pre-event routine to include all the actions to complete prior to your performance.

5. Test out your checklist and pre-event routine and make any additions or adjustments during training or at smaller events so you have refined them before the big event.

MY JOURNEY

Routines definitely tied in with my energy levels and the stress levels that I experienced. I am a creature of habit and I like my routines. Any disruption to my routine sometimes caused some stress. As a result, when I got stressed, my energy levels would dip and so would my ability to run well.

Even for my long Sunday runs, I had my routine for when to get up, what to eat, what stretches I would do before going out the door and get to the run. If I was late getting up, I would feel somewhat stressed and I would rush around trying to squeeze in everything I wanted to do before I got out the door. Those days, my runs were certainly not the best!

Then, when it came to races, some sense of routine helped to calm my nerves and helped me have more energy for the run. Over time, I did look at what worked well and what did not work well for me so that I could streamline my pre-event routine. I subsequently have used this pre-event routine for other race situations and other 'performance' type of events.

Focus

Can you recall a situation when you were so enthralled with something like a movie, a great conversation or reading a good book? Did time just seem to fly by and you didn't notice it passing? Have you ever worked on a really interesting project and before you realized it, the day was gone?

These types of situations where you are not consciously aware of time passing demonstrate an intense focus on something or someone. Yet, the reality is that more often than not, our focus and attention jumps from one thing to the next. According to Gallwey (1981), of the Inner Game series of books, concentration is the most important skill both for outer and inner games. It is the flow of conscious energy of what is going on around you.

Essentially, it is about placing our complete and undivided attention upon objects of our choice. It does take practice, yet with repeated attention, you can learn to develop this skill. Gallwey (1981) identifies the steps for developing concentration and focus. These are discipline, interest, absorption and oneness.

The discipline to pay attention only to the here and now, to what is currently present in your environment is the first step. Interest relates to simply being interested in what you are paying attention to, otherwise why pay attention to it in the first instance. The next step is being absorbed in what you are doing, almost to the exclusion of all else that is going on around you. You are so fully concentrating on what you are doing;

there is no room for any anxiety or fear to enter. This leads onto a sense of 'oneness' and being fully present in the 'Now'. Nothing else is happening except what you are doing. A good example is children focused on a game where they are extremely absorbed and are unaware of the world around them. As athletes, our performance will benefit from developing this same ability to be as absorbed and focused.

How often have you started on one task then picked up something else, before coming back to what you first started? Have you ever tried completing several jobs at once, either at work or at home? Did you have a sense that you were not progressing things? Have you ever been chatting with someone on the phone while checking emails or Facebook?

By the same token, have you ever felt totally absorbed in a task? Did time just seem to fly by? Were you able to exclude any distractions while you got the job done?

All under the pretence of 'multi-tasking', you were actually taking longer to complete tasks than had you been able to focus on one thing at a time and complete it. In a performance situation, the ability to focus on one thing at a time, or rather focus only on task-relevant things will make a big difference to the outcomes you achieve because all your energy, attention, and efforts are directed towards a desired outcome.

WHY FOCUS ON YOUR FOCUS?

When you are able to place 100% of your focus and attention on what you need to do to perform, you are effectively helping yourself to perform even better. Orlick (2000, p. 50) says "when you are focused in sport, you are totally connected to what you are engaged in, to the exclusion of everything else. In a very real sense, you and your performance become one, and nothing else in the world exists for that period of time".

Your ability to shut out distractions and not let them affect you, thereby keeping a razor-sharp focus on what you need to do, certainly helps rather than hinders your performance abilities. Having a tunnel-like vision on everything you need to think about and do will positively affect your ability to perform.

The first step is identifying what is relevant and important to pay attention to. These 'task-relevant' things are your thoughts and where you place your attention as well as your actions and what you do. These thoughts and actions need to help, rather than hinder, your performance. For example, dwelling on the other competitors and what they are doing will do nothing to boost your own performance whereas focusing just on yourself will help you.

To help develop your awareness, write out a list of the thoughts that you generally have leading up to and including your performance. Then, take a look and evaluate them to determine whether they help or hinder your performance abilities. *Do they give you a boost and are focused solely on you or do they drag you away from your own efforts?* If they help, then they are likely to be task-relevant.

The next step is developing the habit of keeping your focus and your attention solely on those task-relevant things and coming up with strategies to deal with any distractions. Inevitably, there will be distractions that take your attention away from what you are doing – be they other competitors in the event, something at home that you need to do or a challenging situation you are currently experiencing. Once you notice your attention has strayed to thoughts that are not related to your performance, you need to bring them back to the task in hand. For example, how you are feeling in your body is a task-relevant thing to be aware of for a race, whereas worrying about the other competitors and how they are doing does not help you perform any better and is not considered a task-relevant thing.

Like any other habit, it is a question of becoming aware and noticing when it is happening, and then gently bringing yourself back on track. With practice, the habit of maintaining focus on what is important will become second nature and the ability to refocus after a distraction will become easier to do.

To help you understand task-relevant thoughts and actions, let us next explore the different types of focus and the effects on performance.

DIFFERENT TYPES OF FOCUS

We all focus on different things at different times and our attention, concentration and focus skills are continually shifting. Depending on the activity in which you want to perform at peak levels, your focus might need to shift between narrow or broad, and internal or external. Nideffer (1976) described these different attention styles in his Test of Attentional and Interpersonal Style (TAIS).

Narrow focus is simply the concentration of your attention on what you are doing and where you are going. It is as if you are oblivious to what else is going on around you. Broad focus is being aware of everything that is going on around you. It is almost like having a sixth sense of what is going to happen next in the play. Internal focus is putting your attention on what is happening inside you, being more aware of what happens within your body and your own thoughts. External focus is being aware of what others are doing and wondering what they are thinking.

For example, in a running context, simply focusing on yourself and what you do, almost disregarding what is happening around you, can increase your performance. Whereas in a team sport, if you focused solely on yourself, you might not be an effective team player! Ideally, players should be alert and aware of what is going on around them, how the play is developing, and what other players are doing.

Let us now look at each type of focus and consider what might work in different scenarios.

With a Broad / External focus, individuals will have a greater awareness of a wide range of external stimuli. Individuals take in the whole picture of what is going on and are able to assess situations, read and react to non-verbal clues and react instinctively to the environment. They have a good 'street sense' and are better skilled in fast-moving sports.

A Broad/Internal type of focus applies to those who are good at organizing, planning, and integrating a wide range of internal details such as thoughts, ideas, feelings and experiences. They are good at analyzing, planning and problem solving. These individuals usually develop strategies, analyze opponents and plan training programmes.

A Narrow/External type of concentration is used when individuals are very focused on the action they are about to do, almost to the exclusion of external stimuli. This might be a player executing a move such as kicking a ball, making a golf putt or hitting a tennis ball. They focus on the detail of what they are doing and aim for perfection in the execution.

A Narrow/Internal type of concentration applies to those who are very focused on the 'here and now' method of dealing with situations. Those with this tendency would mentally prepare for situations. They would go through the motions in their head by rehearsing what they are going to do and how they are going to do it.

Each individual has a preferred style of focus and concentration. Yet, by becoming aware of which concentration zone you tend to fall into is a good starting point. From this place of awareness, you can then determine if that particular zone works best for you and whether you could benefit from shifting zones at different points during your performance.

In your performance situation, where does your concentration and focus need to be? If you have a general tendency to have one type of focus, yet when you are performing you need another, you will need to remain aware of this and monitor what is going on. The table below provides a graphical representation using different sports to show the different concentration zones.

Figure 3 : Concentration Styles

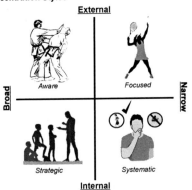

Take for example a rugby match. As the game evolves, the players need to be in the Broad/External zone to be able to take in how the play develops. As they catch the ball, they need to switch to Narrow/External focus to either throw the ball or run for the touchline. They need to quickly, almost instantaneously, go to the Broad/ Internal area to decide how best to play the situation based on experience and then return to the Narrow /External to execute it. They quickly switch between concentration zones without realizing it and the quicker they do that, the better they will perform.

At any point in time, the athlete will shift their focus of concentration into one of the four areas. Appreciating that there are different zones of focus is one element that can help you develop stronger focus and concentration skills because you can start to recognize where you most comfortably sit and whether it is appropriate for what you are doing. You also need to be aware that your level of stress will also affect your ability to focus and concentrate.

HOW STRESS AFFECTS CONCENTRATION

As human beings, we like to stay with what we know and what is comfortable. As stress and pressure increase, we have a tendency to retreat to our comfort zone. Therefore, recognizing whether you have broad or narrow, external or internal tendencies is a good starting point because your comfort zone may, or may not, be appropriate for your performance situation.

If for example, your tendency is to stay within the Narrow/Internal concentration area, and the demands of the situation are broad and external, then retreating to your comfort zone does not help you to be effective in the situation. If however, you were in a different situation where Narrow/Internal concentration were beneficial and you needed to think of the next best course of action, then having that tendency would be fine. Appreciating that we all have different comfort zones in regards to our concentration and focus, we can then develop our awareness of where we place our attention in order to recognize and shift concentration zones when necessary.

You can start to develop this awareness by simply stopping what you are doing and paying attention to what and where you are paying attention. *Is your focus on the big picture or the detail? Is your focus on things external or internal to you?* By developing this awareness in everyday situations, you can then more easily use these skills during your training sessions and more importantly, in your events. By noticing where your attention is, you can then begin to see situations where you might need a different kind of attention and shift your focus to an appropriate concentration zone as the situation demands.

By noticing what you are noticing, you will more easily recognize where your attention may be and determine whether it is appropriate for the given situation. Notice what happens when you start feeling stressed about something. *Where does your attention go? Is it internal or external? Is it broad or narrow?* For some individuals, their focus and attention retreats to Narrow/Internal and they focus on their own thoughts and fears. Yet if they were able to bring their attention to outside themselves, they may not become so worried or stressed.

In addition to stress affecting our concentration, it also affects our performance. Nideffer (1976) demonstrates the effects of stress on performances in the below table.

Figure 4 : Effect of Pressure on Performance

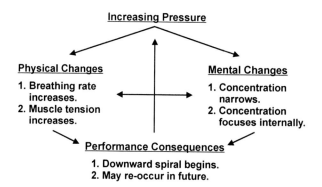

Therefore, it is important to deal with any stressor in order to help improve performance.

DEALING WITH DISTRACTIONS

It is inevitable that you will encounter many distractions prior to and during your performance. Yet, learning how to deal with distractions will help you to maintain your tunnel-like vision on doing what is necessary to be the best you can be.

Distractions might be people, places or things that do not help you reach your goals. Paying attention to these distractions will most likely increase your stress levels and might not help you actually perform well. Effectively, focus on those things that you can control and let go of those things that you have no control over. For example, in a running event, focusing on the other competitors and those who are better than you does nothing towards helping you run any better.

Whereas focusing on yourself, your strength, your foot strike, even your breathing does indeed help you.

By becoming clear on the things that help your performance, those task-relevant details, you can help yourself stay focused on them. However, your mind may at times wander off to non task-relevant things because that is human nature. By quickly noticing when your thoughts are on non task-related things and bringing your attention back on track, you help yourself to perform more effectively. Saying that, there may be times where it is important to 'switch off' and not focus on task-relevant details. An example could be a golfer who needs to switch off as they walk down the fairway towards their ball. As soon as they are about to address the ball, they need to refocus on the task in hand.

One way to practise this focus on task-related things is during your training sessions. Challenge yourself to pay attention to one thing during your practice. It could be anything that contributes to your efforts. In the case of a runner, they could focus on their breathing or their posture. In the case of a golfer, they could focus on how stable their hips are during the swing. The focus area will be different for each athlete or performer. Decide what you want to focus on and each time you notice that you are not paying attention to this element, bring yourself back on track and refocus on what you have chosen to pay attention to. With practice, the noticing and the refocusing do become easier.

In dealing with distractions, pain in the body could be one of the distractions you experience. Pain is the body's way of trying to tell you that not all is well. Yet, deciding whether this pain can be dismissed or paid attention to is up to each individual. If the pain is serious, then you obviously need to pay attention to it and do something about it. This might mean that you have to stop what you are doing immediately before further damage occurs. However, if the pain is not serious it might be the body's way of telling you that you are simply pushing the comfort zones. For example, runners might feel a stitch in their side, yet concentrating on their breathing can minimize that.

As the saying goes, 'What you resist, persists' so in the case of an annoying distraction in your own body, simply acknowledge it and then place your attention on something else. Almost as if you say to your body, 'OK, I hear you, yet I'm busy right now doing my race and I choose to focus on being at my best.' Then, make sure you place your attention on yourself and what helps you perform even better. A runner might focus on their stride or their bounce, a cyclist might focus on the smoothness of their legs or a swimmer might focus on the pull of their stroke. Whenever an athlete chooses to focus on a small detail of their actions, the distracting niggle in the body seems to disappear. In addition, your conscious brain can only focus on one thing at a time, so make sure that it is something positive and helpful to you!

LETTING GO OF MISTAKES

Dwelling on mistakes is a focus issue. When some players make a mistake they dwell on it and beat themselves up internally or somehow act it out externally. They might have missed a penalty shot, fouled a ball or missed a putt, and then they seem to lose it. They are unable to regain their composure and play effectively and as a result, continue making even more mistakes. They have effectively held onto that mistake and not let it go. They might even spiral downwards, their performance getting increasingly worse.

153

What often happens is that these individuals are focusing on the mistake and not moving on. Therefore, during a performance, it is important to be present in the moment and let go of any previous mistakes or mishaps. Dwelling on the past, dwelling on the fact that they missed an easy shot, fumbled a ball or was offside, does not do the player or the team any good.

A golfer would need to focus on each individual shot they take, rather than dwell on the missed putt from the previous hole. A football player might focus on the developing play rather than dwelling on missing the pass to another player or fouling the penalty shot they just took. Dwelling on the mistake is as if you are running forward yet at the same time, you are looking over your shoulder to see where you have come from. Although you still move forward, it is at a slower pace than if you simply faced forward and looked where you were going. Dwelling on the past, thinking about what you just did or didn't do or what you could have said differently are all things that bring your attention effectively behind you to what has passed.

Even if these glances are literal or metaphorical, and only momentary, you are still shifting your focus and attention away from the direction you want to be going and that is forward! Essentially, focus on where you are going and what you want, rather than on where you have come from or what you do not want.

FOCUS IS LIKE MEDITATION

For those of you who do meditation, you will know that the key is refocusing the mind to where you are placing your attention for that meditation session. Perhaps you focus on a sound, on your breath or the flame of a candle. For many of us, even though we intend to focus on one thing, random thoughts pop into our mind like what we have to do later, what we are going to eat or even the discussion we just had. Once we realize that our attention has wandered, we have to consciously bring our focus back. Even with repeated practice of paying attention to one thing, our thoughts may jump in from time to time. The skill is in acknowledging these thoughts when they do appear and then bringing our attention back to what we were initially focusing on.

To start this practice and to develop the skill of focusing, a simple practice is to sit quietly for one minute, then two three, four, then five minutes, and focus on one thing and one thing only. Try right it now.

Simply focus on 10 breaths, placing 100% of your attention on your in breath and your out breath. *How easy or challenging was that?* For many of you, random thoughts might have popped up even though you were trying to focus on only 10 breaths. This demonstrates how challenging it can be to focus on one thing and only one thing.

Similarly, when you try to focus on your game, your performance and your efforts, random thoughts will most likely pop up. *If you find it challenging to focus on taking 10 breaths, what do you think is going on when you try to focus for the duration of a match or a race?* Yet, like any skill, you can improve your ability to focus with practice. By practising outside the performance arena where your stress levels are lower and distractions are fewer, you will more easily be able to call upon this skill when you need it during your performances.

Orlick (2000) suggests some ideas to help you focus.

- Use your imagination to feel yourself execute the movement of your sport and then do the action. Allow your body to simply perform the action, without any thought.

155

- Focus totally on connecting, physically and mentally, with each move you make.
- In team sports or competing against an opponent, practise becoming aware of your environment, before returning your attention to connecting with your actions.
- Work on holding your entire focus for short periods of time, and then gradually increase that time.

Additionally, practising meditation can help you develop your ability to focus for your performances. It helps you to develop the skill to place your attention on one thing and to let random thoughts go. By practising this during quiet times, you start to strengthen your ability to do the same during a busier and stressful time such as a performance event.

SUMMARY

Focus does indeed contribute to helping you be the best you can be, and it is a skill that can be developed through practice. Wherever you put your attention, your body will follow. Focus on what you want rather than what you do not want.

By recognizing where you have strong focus and concentration and what concentration zone you tend to find the most comfortable is a first step. From there, you can start developing the skill and strategies to focus in an appropriate zone when you need it the most.

You may begin to notice a pattern of where you are most comfortable and in what different times and situations it shifts. From there, you can assess whether it is appropriate for your given performance scenario and do something about it.

Developing the ability to switch your focus and concentration when and where you need it can help you. It helps you because all the noise and distractions – whether they be external influences or internal self-talk - hamper your ability to be the best you can be. Having the awareness and flexibility to switch to an appropriate mode of focus and concentration will help you shift to a zone that is better for your performance.

It is obvious that stress has a negative impact on your abilities to focus and concentrate. Therefore, you need to practise your refocusing strategies much like meditation practice, to be able to more easily notice when your thoughts have wandered and bring them back on track. It takes some practice and at times it is more challenging than at other times; however, by learning to develop the skill of focus will contribute to increased performance abilities. By having strong focus when you want to perform, you direct your attention and energy to the outcome you desire.

Overall, the importance of focus means that all your attention is on task-relevant things that support you and help you perform to the best of your abilities. Effectively, focus on the process of what you are doing and what you need to do, rather than on the outcome you want to achieve or other things going on around you.

STEPS SUMMARY

1. Identify the types of thoughts you have when you perform.

2. Determine whether the thoughts are task-relevant thoughts. *Do they help or hinder your performance abilities?*

157

3. If you make a mistake, let it go, refocus on the task in hand and focus on what will help you perform.

4. Be present in what you are doing by being 100% engaged and focused on what you need to do and how you are feeling as you execute the moves.

MY JOURNEY

Initially, my thoughts and my focus were all over the place! Yet, because of my weaken energy reserves, it became critical for me to manage my thoughts and where I placed my attention in order to be able to do all that I wanted to do, particularly on those long runs.

Therefore, I continually had to ask myself whether what I was doing, or what I was thinking about, helped or hindered me. Was it boosting me up, or was it draining me? This continual self-questioning helped me to identify those 'task-relevant' thoughts and actions to ensure that I helped myself stay focused and on task.

I would also beat myself up at times for making mistakes, for doing something that I perceived was wrong or that was not good enough. Yet again, all these thoughts would make me feel drained and lose what precious energy I had available. I quickly learned that I needed to let go of mistakes rather than dwell on them because I knew I wasn't helping myself to run effectively.

The cliché: 'What is past is past, and you can not change it' became almost like a mantra to help me let go of those mistakes or let go of those thoughts that did not serve me. The repeated practice of focusing on what I was doing and on thoughts and actions that

---

supported me, helped to develop the practice of being present in the 'Now'.

It was challenging to *not* think about the 101 things to do at home, about the fears of what lay ahead of me, about things I had said or done previously. Yet I soon learned that all those thoughts were not helping me run any better or any faster. They were, in effect, dragging me down and draining me of my energy. What helped was focusing on positive, uplifting thoughts and on my running.

Focusing on what I aimed to do, focusing on my running style, focusing on the scenery around me, all helped me to stay 'in the moment' and present to what I was doing. For me, the incentive was my energy levels because when I was not present, I would feel more tired and drained.

Post Event Review

The previous steps all contribute towards you raising your performance abilities to greater heights. If you are going to put yourself into a similar situation in the future, it is best to complete this last step in this *Winning Strategies* process. A **Post-Event Review** completes the peak performance cycle. This review contributes towards helping you do even better the next time you have a similar event and when you want to improve your results.

The first step in your review is to re-assess the original goals you set for yourself. You then review your mental preparation, followed by all the skills and techniques you adopt when performing at events. By completing an objective review, you can identify what worked well and what did not work well.

Ideally, at your next performance, you will repeat the things that worked well and avoid the things that did not work well. Each time you go through this process for your performance you can refine, re-adjust and realign what you need to do to improve.

Overall, this helps you to raise your game and your performances to greater heights each time you go out.

Review, Reflect and Plan

Once you have finished a big event, you can sit back with your feet resting comfortably. You have done all the hard work and you have done what you set out to do. Give yourself a pat on the back for putting in the hard work – regardless of the outcome.

The results may, or may not, be what you expected. The important thing to do is to maintain a positive and balanced perspective. Maintaining an objective perspective may at times be challenging, particularly immediately after the event where emotions may be running high. It is therefore important to take some time out before you look into the details and the factors that contributed to your performance.

Great performances are very satisfying! So, by identifying the elements that contributed to that level of performance enables you to repeat the pattern at the next event or the next performance. Even great performances and great results can be improved upon! Known as 'modelling excellence' in NLP terms, you can examine closely the elements that contributed to your great performance. In this post-event review, you can model your own excellence in order to create your unique 'recipe for success'.

Additionally, by identifying the elements that may have negatively affected your performance you will have the information you need to make changes to improve for the future. Rather than beat yourself up about what you did wrong, explore ways to do things differently the next time. *What adjustments could you make, what variations could you implement in either your training or your strategic approach to the event?*

Use this knowledge into yourself, your training and your performance to adjust what you did before so that you achieve even better results the next time.

WHY REVIEW?

There are many factors that contribute to the results you achieved and sometimes these results are what you expected, while at other times they are not. By taking some time to review what worked well and what did not work well, you can identify the elements that contributed to your outcome. Effectively, you are creating your own 'recipe for success' whereby you have all the ingredients to ensure you get the desired outcome. In the same way you follow a recipe to bake a cake or create a dish for dinner, you can create your own recipe for your performances. Grout and Perrin (2004) suggest that the key element of all top-sporting champions is that they learn from their mistakes as well as their successes.

Once you know the elements that contributed to your performance results, you can then identify which elements to change and, therefore, develop a plan of action to help you prepare for your next event or for the next season. These changes in your routine and changes in your preparation are all in view of achieving different results. There may be some things that you can adjust, you can tweak or you can practise during training so that you can easily and effortlessly use them during a performance event.

So let us examine the best time to do this review and some of the things you need to take into account.

COMPLETING THE REVIEW

As human beings, we often have selective memories. We might overlook some of the obvious things we did well or perhaps the obvious things we did not do so well. Alternatively, we might be overly critical of the minute details and be harsh on ourselves.

When you finish your event, you may be feeling fantastic and on a high because of the results you achieved were what you expected or perhaps even better. On the other hand, you may be feeling somewhat low and in a negative mindset because the results you achieved were not what you had anticipated. Whatever the case may be and how you feel, it is not wise to complete a thorough and detailed review immediately after a big event.

It is therefore important to put in some time and space between your actual performance and your review. This will help you to have a more objective view on things. Wait a few days before sitting down to evaluate, assess and review all the elements that contributed to your performance. In addition, talking through your review with a trusted coach or friend will provide an outside perspective on what you did. Also, bouncing ideas around with another person can help to generate new ways of thinking about what you can do differently the next time.

Many factors contribute to your performance results. Essentially, your review needs to look at what you did to achieve the results you achieved, what worked well and what didn't work so well. Then, make a plan for the next event. *What can you repeat the next time? Where can you make some adjustments? What can you eliminate for the next time?* Remember that everything you do, be it sports-related or otherwise, contribute towards your performances and the outcomes you achieve during your event. So, make sure you keep things in perspective within the big picture of your life.

Let us take a closer look at all the elements that have contributed towards your performances and start at the very beginning of the Winning Strategies process.

IN THE BEGINNING ...

The initial steps in your review are to help you get a big picture perspective before going into the details of what worked well and what could be changed for the next time. This information will help you to identify elements to put into your own 'recipe for success' to achieve personal peak performances for the future.

To kick-start your review and to help you create that big picture, here are some questions to ponder.

- *What are you doing now that **you can continue** doing in order to perform at your best?*
- *What are you doing now that **you have to stop** doing in order to perform at your best?*
- *What are you not doing now that **you could be doing** in order to perform at your best?*

Once you have this general view, it is helpful to get into the detail of what specifically contributed to your results. This review goes through the steps outlined in this Winning Strategies peak performance process.

GETTING STARTED ... FOR THE NEXT TIME

Goals and outcomes

- Did you establish clearly defined, and written out, SMART goals? Were they Specific, Measurable, Achievable, Realistic and Timely? Were they stated positively?

166

- Did you have several goals in relation to the overall big goal? The more goals you have, the more opportunities to 'tick the boxes' for success that you have indeed achieved them.
- Did you set performance goals, rather than outcome goals? You have personal control over performance goals, whereas outcome goals, such as a specific time or placing, you do not have control over.

Values and beliefs

- What are the reasons you are doing what you are doing?
- What benefits will achieving the outcome give you?
- What do you need to believe in order to do what you want to do?
- Where might you have some limiting beliefs and how can you dispel them?

Self-management

- What people, places and things drain your energy? Which ones make you feel uplifted or recharged?
- What mechanisms can you put in place to minimize the negative effects of what drains you?
- How can you ensure you have sufficient contact with those things that help you feel recharged?
- How effective were your personal boundaries in managing your time, energy and attention? What could you do differently?

Life balance

- Looking at all important areas in your life, how does your goal fit with the other areas and other roles and responsibilities?
- Are there any adjustments needed to either your priorities or to the time you spend on different activities?
- Do you need to create clearer boundaries between different areas of your life in order to do your preparation and training, and do people know about them?
- Can you enlist the help and support of someone, which enables you to more easily do what you need to do?

MENTAL PREPARATION ... FLEXING YOUR MUSCLES

Confidence

- How confident were you feeling before events that went well? What about when things turned out not so well?
- What sort of people, places or things had a positive or negative influence on your confidence?
- What does the feeling of confidence look and feel like to you? Imagine what it is like. Imagine your posture, how you are standing, how you are moving and what sort of things you are saying to yourself.
- Can you review and remind yourself of all the positive, uplifting, confidence-boosting experiences that you have included in your confidence resumé?

Internal dialogue

- What sort of things do you say to yourself? It is helpful to actually write these down so you can see, rather than simply hear, what is being said?
- How can you turn any negative commentary to something more positive and supportive? What sort of things could you say instead?
- Were there particular situations where there was more internal chatter? Less internal chatter? Recognizing the situations and being prepared for them can help you manage it.

Mental rehearsal

- How often did you visualise your performance before your event and what sort of aspects were contained in your visualisation? How can you increase the intensity of the experience from your visualisation?
- How vivid was your visualisation? Did you rehearse rich experiences including what you would feel like, what you would see and hear?
- What type of scenarios can you include when handling difficult situations such as when things are not going to plan or as expected? Imagine the experiences and imagine yourself handling them easily and effortlessly.

EVENT PERFORMANCE ... SWITCHING IT ON

Relaxation

- What can you do to remain calm and relaxed prior to and during your event? How does this feel in each major part of your body?

- When you notice an increase in tension, what can you do to relax?
- Do any people, places or things increase, or decrease, your sense of stress and tension? What can you do to help yourself remain calm and relaxed?
- Where can you practise more of the relaxation exercises? Make sure you practise them outside the pressured event arena so you know they work and can call upon them when necessary.

Routines

- What did you include in your pre-event checklist and routine? Any changes that could be made?
- How effective was using your pre-event checklist to how you felt and how you performed?
- In what ways did your routine help you get physically and mentally prepared for your event? How did you feel going into the race?

Focus

- What are the task-relevant things to place your attention on?
- Why type of focus is most needed in your performance? Broad or narrow? Internal or external?
- What strategies do you have in place to minimize or deal with distractions?
- Who can you ask to help and support you in maintaining your focus – be that for training or during competitions?

SUMMARY

A review of all the elements that contributed to your performance is beneficial after you have completed your event to help you improve for the next time. It is important, however, to take some time out before you undertake this review so that you can complete it in a more objective manner. Your judgement may not be as objective as possible soon after an event when emotions, either high or low, may be coursing through you. You may either be too critical and harsh about the 'mistakes' you made or so overjoyed that you omit to see anything that could be improved for the next time.

Every step in the peak performance process – from goal setting and motivation, your values and beliefs, even your confidence, focus and mental rehearsal – all come into play and will affect your performance. It is like looking under a microscope where every element is minutely examined. You benefit from examining everything in great detail that contributed to the outcome you achieved.

This review is to help you pick out the best things so that you can repeat them again. Additionally, it can help you identify elements that didn't work so well for you and that could be modified or omitted the next time. Overall, a review helps you understand what contributed to the outcome you achieved and helps you to improve for future events.

Quite simply put, *what can you do to make your next performance even better?* The answers will help you to make a plan, make adjustments and then put them into action to help you raise your game!

My Journey

Once I had completed my first marathon, I caught the bug to do more! My review of what I did was partly motivated by the fact that I had the incentive to regain my physical health almost as if I were proving that I could re-join the human race. I also wanted to see what might be different if I did another marathon when I was healthier and more robust. What could be different? How might things change?

On this first occasion, my incentive to eat really healthy food and take care of myself was motivated by the fact that if I did not, I would be unable to work or do the marathon training. For the next time, I already had the experience of running a marathon so I knew I could do it as long as I followed a prescribed training programme that progressively and safely built up the mileage. Because my health had improved, I was less strict with taking care of my physical health yet still paid attention to it.

All of this did not take into account the fact that I injured my back in a fall on my last long run before my marathon. Although I still completed this second marathon in Toronto in 2002, I certainly experienced quite a bit of pain and discomfort during the last few miles! Yet, I was determined to still cross the finish line, and I did!

I appreciated the importance of exploring all the elements that went into the first achievement in order to take the good bits, let go of the bad bits and modify things to see whether the changes would help or hinder my future achievements.

This review was similar to the 'post- event reviews' that used to be conducted at work after big exercises. These reviews consisted of looking at all the experiences, responses and actions during the exercise to determine whether they would be the same if the exercise were to be repeated. Any recommendations were taken into consideration for future exercises.

I have also used elements of this Winning Strategies process for other performance situations such as delivering a big presentation or going for a job interview. I most certainly needed to boost my confidence levels going into these stressful situations and had to manage the negative internal dialogue. I also mentally rehearsed how I wanted things to progress and even thought of some pre-event checklists and routines that could help reduce my nervousness, in addition to some 'one conscious breath' relaxation exercises.

Overall, I have used all of these elements in so many different aspects and situations in my life!

Conclusion

The journey towards raising your performances is an exciting and challenging one! You can do all the technical preparation, have the physical capabilities, and still achieve great results. Additionally, by considering the mental preparation aspects, you can achieve outstanding results. It does, however, still take practice; it still takes effort; it still takes consistent vigilance to monitor your thoughts and train them towards helping you be the best you can be.

It is important to recognize that your peak performance levels may be very different from another person's levels. We are all so different and so unique. For one person, their goal may be monumental whereas for another person, it is simply like a warm-up. As an example, take someone just recovering from a serious injury. For them, simply being able to walk unaided or run around the track without any discomfort may be a major milestone.

From the initial step of getting started and deciding to 'go for it', you can benefit from clarifying your goals, your motivation, your values and beliefs as well as identifying how a particular goal fits in with other important areas in your life. Ensuring you maintain a healthy balance in all your activities and responsibilities contributes towards you having the time and energy to devote to your preparation. These initial steps are the foundations for your journey towards achieving peak performance levels.

All the mental preparation you do beforehand will influence your outcome so focusing on the mind element

175

will help. Being mentally prepared for your event means you develop increased confidence in what you are going to do. You can turn down the volume or put on mute any negative self-talk and turn up the volume on the positive supportive comments. You can also mentally rehearse your entire event from start to finish, as if you are directing your own movie where you are the producer. This tricks the brain to thinking that it has already done the performance. So, when you get to your event, your brain thinks it has already 'been there and done that'!

Then, on the big day, you need to be switched on. Developing the ability to relax and to use one conscious breath will help you calm those nerves, clear your head and perform even better. Developing routines helps because you can go on autopilot and do not have to think too much about what you are doing … you simply do it. Also, knowing what to focus on and knowing what task-relevant things help you to perform, you can let go of mistakes and focus on simply doing what you need to do.

Once you have completed your event, it is important to take time out to recognize your achievements and take what learning you can from the experience. By reviewing and reflecting on what you accomplished and identifying the elements that contributed to the results, you can then develop a template or 'recipe for success' for the next time.

Now, consider where else you would like to achieve peak levels of performance. You can take all that you have learnt throughout this *Winning Strategies* process and then apply it to other areas where you want to be the best you can be. Whether it is when you are working on a big project or about to make a big presentation at work, going for an interview, conducting an important meeting or having a major discussion with someone ... you can use some, or even all, of the steps to help you be the best you can be for that particular situation.

Using these Winning Strategies steps will help create a mindset for success and help align your thoughts, your actions, and your energy towards realizing your greatest potential. With every training session and every day, consider what you are doing and how you are doing it.

Do your actions contribute towards supporting you to be the very best at all times? Do they help or hinder your progress towards your goal?

It does take practice and vigilance yet with attention and regular effort, you can do it; you can develop your mental toughness skills and be like a gold medal winner!

MY JOURNEY

My journey, w h i c h started with me becoming ill and then completing my first marathon in 3h56m less than a year later, was the beginning of much soul searching of what I was doing and where I was going.

This ultimately led me to changing careers and becoming a mental performance and lifestyle coach. The experiences that I had during that particular journey, and countless others after that, helped me to understand and appreciate that we all have different challenges to face.

What might be a major challenge for one person seems like only a minor thing to another. Yet, by maintaining a positive approach and a clear focus on an end destination, the journey is so much more enjoyable and easier!

CONCLUSION

Winning Strategies Summary

Here is a checklist to summarize the Winning Strategies process.

Getting Started

Goals and motivation	What do you want to achieve and what benefits will you gain?	
Values and beliefs	What is important about achieving this goal and what difference in your life will it make? What do you need to believe to achieve it?	
Self-management	How can you maximize the positive effect of people, places and things that help you perform? How can you minimize any negatives?	
Life balance	How does your goal fit with the other important areas in your life? Does anything need to shift?	

Mental Preparation

Confidence	What does confidence look and feel like to you, and how could you tap into it for your performance?	

| Internal dialogue | How can you turn up the volume on the positive things you say? How can you mute or dispel any negative things? | |
| Mental rehearsal | How real can your movie be of you performing at your best? What do you see, hear and feel? | |

Event Performance

Relaxation	How can you maintain a sense of relaxation? What do you need to remember to take one conscious breath?	
Routines	What is contained in your pre-event checklist and routine? What things can you keep, alter or discard for the next time?	
Focus	What are the task-relevant elements that help you perform? How can you bring your attention back to them?	

Post Event Review

| Review, reflect and plan | What can be repeated the next time and what could be modified? | |

About Midgie

Canadian-born mental performance coach, Midgie Thompson specializes in 'Inspiring Excellence' in individuals and teams. She helps develop performance skills by combining mental toughness techniques with balanced lifestyle choices.

Midgie founded Bright Futures Coaching Ltd in 2003 and has been providing motivational, mental performance and personal development coaching ever since. The company also offers business performance, management and communication skills courses.

Midgie regularly writes for sporting and business journals, and is a media spokesperson on mental preparation skills, peak performance, goal setting, motivation and confidence building. She also teaches at the University of Brighton and provides coaching and advice to Mind Tools™ Career Excellence Club.

She has coached athletes at all levels from amateur to world championship, and worked with people in the business world up to managing director level.

Midgie lives in Brighton, UK, and is a year-round open water swimmer and recreational triathlete.

Contacting the author

If you would like some help, encouragement and support to implement these skills, strategies and techniques, contact Midgie by

Email: midgie@brightfuturescoaching.com

Or call: +44 (0) 1273 906 216 (UK)

+1 704 557 0126 (US)

Midgie is available for motivational and keynote speeches and workshops worldwide.

SOCIAL MEDIA

Connect with Midgie via social media.

Twitter: MidgieThompson

LinkedIn: Midgie Thompson

Facebook:
http://www.facebook.com/BrightFuturesCoaching

References

American Psychological Association (2013) *The Road to Resilience* [online] <http://www.apa.org/helpcenter/road- resilience.aspx> [date accessed 10 January 2013]

Bull, S. (2006) *The Game Plan*, Chichester, UK: Capstone Publishing Ltd

Butler, G. and Hope, T. (1995), *Manage Your Mind*, Oxford, UK: Oxford University Press

Dahlkoetter, J. (2003) *Your Performing Edge*, 3rd edition, San Carlos, California, US: Pulgas Ridge Press

Gallwey, W.T. (1981) *The Inner Game of Golf*, New York, US: Random House Inc.

Garratt, T. (1999) *Sporting Excellence*, Carmarthen, Wales, UK: Crown House Publishing Ltd

Grout, J. and Perrin, S. (2004) *Mind Games*, Chichester, UK: Capstone Publishing Ltd

Jones, G. and Moorhouse, A. (2007) *Developing Mental Toughness*, Oxford, UK: Spring Hill

Lazarus, J. (2006) *Ahead of the Game*, Cornwall, UK: Ecademy Press

Loehr, J. and Schwartz, T. (2003) *On Form*, London, UK: Nicholas Brealey Publishing

Lynch, J. and Scott, W (1999) *Running Within*, Ontario, Canada: Human Kinetics

Mind Tools (2013) *Locke's Goal Setting Theory* [online] <http://www.mindtools.com/pages/article/newHTE_ 87.htm> [date accessed 3 January 2013]

Mind Tools (2012) *Stress and Your Performance* [online] <http://www.mindtools.com/stress/UnderstandStress /StressPerformance.htm> [date accessed 6/12/2012]

Nideffer, R. (1976) Test of attentional and interpersonal style, *Journal of Personality and Social Psychology*, Vol. 34(3), September 1976, 394–404

O'Connor, J. (2001) *NLP Workbook*, London, UK: Element, Harper Collins Publishers Ltd

Orlick, T. (1998) *Embracing your Potential*, Ontario, Canada: Human Kinetics

Orlick, T. (2000) *In Pursuit of Excellence*, Ontario, Canada: Human Kinetics

Porter, K. (2003) *The Mental Athlete*, Ontario, Canada: Human Kinetics

Richardson, C. (2000) *Take Time for Your Life*, London, UK: Random House

Bibliography

Bandura, A. (1973) "Self-Efficacy: Towards a Unifying Theory of Behavioural Change" *Psychology Review*, 84, p 191–215

Baum, K. and Trubo, R. (1999) *The Mental Edge*, New York, US: The Berkley Publishing Group

Bokeno, R.M. (2009) Genius of learning relationships: mentoring and coaching as communicative interaction, *Development and Learning in Organizations*. Vol. 23, No. 1, p5–8

Boyd, E. and Fales, A. (1983) Reflective Learning, *Journal of Humanistic Psychology*, Vol. 23, No. 2, p99–117

Brockbank, A. & McGill, I. (2006) *Facilitating Reflective Learning Through Mentoring & Coaching*. London, UK: Kogan Press

Brockbank, A., McGill, I. and Beech, N. (2002) *Reflective Learning in Practice.* Aldershot, UK: Gower Publishing Ltd

Charvet, S.R. (1997) *Words That Change Minds*, 2nd edition, Iowa, US: Kendall/Hunt Publishing Company

Clutterbuck, D. (2003) *Managing work-life balance: a guide for HR in achieving organisational and individual change.* London, UK: Chartered Institute of Personnel and Development

Covey, S. (1989) *The 7 Habits of Highly Effective People.* London, UK: Simon & Schuster

Downey, M. (1999) *Effective Coaching.* London, UK: Texere Publishing Ltd

Evolution Training (2003) NLP Diploma, Practitioner and Master Practitioner [course notes]. Chichester, UK: Unpublished

Gallwey. W.T. (1974) *The Inner Game of Tennis.* New York, US: Random House

Gallwey. W.T. (2000) *The Inner Game of Work.* New York, US: Random House

Garratt, T. (1999) *Sporting Excellence – Optimising Sports Performance Using NLP.* Wales, UK: Crown House Publishing Ltd

Garvey, B. (1994) What is Mentoring? *Education & Training,* Vol. 36, No. 5, p.4–7

Haime, J. (2010) *You are a Contender,* New York, US: Morgan James, The Entrepreneurial Publisher

Irvine, D. (2003) *Becoming Real,* Florida, US: DC Press

Katie, Byron (2002) *Loving What Is: Four Questions That Can Change Your Life,* London, UK: Rider Books

Leary-Joyce, J. (2009) *The Psychology of Success,* Harlow, UK: Pearson Education Ltd

Lynch, J. (2006) *The Way of the Champion,* Vermont, US: Tuttle Publishing

Megginson, D. and Clutterbuck, D. (1995) *Mentoring in Action.* London, UK: Kogan Page

Phillips, R. (1996) Coaching for Performance, *Employee Counselling Today.* Vol. 8, No. 4, p29–32

Richardson, C. (2009) *The Art of Extreme Self-Care,* London, UK: Hay House UK Ltd

Robbins, A. (1992) *Awaken the Giant Within*, New Jersey, US: Simon and Schuster

Rotella, B. (1995) *Golf is not the game of perfect*, New York, US: Simon & Schuster

Schneider, B.D. (2008) *Energy Leadership*, New Jersey, US: John Wiley & Sons Inc.

Schwartz, T., Gomes, J. and McCarthy, C. (2010) *Be Excellent at Anything,* London, UK: Simon & Schuster Ltd

Seligman, M. (2011) *Flourish*, London, UK: Nicholas Brealey Publishing

Skiffington, S. and Zeus, P. (2004) *Behavioural Coaching,* Australia: McGraw Hill

Spackman, K. (2009) *The Winners Bible*, North Carolina, US: The Winners Institute LLC

Terry, R. and Churches, R. (2009) *The NLP Toolkit,* Carmarthen, Wales, UK: Crown House Publishing Ltd

Whitmore, J.K. (2002) *Coaching for Performance: Growing People, Performance and Purpose.* London, UK: Nicholas Brealey Publishing

Zeus, P. and Skiffington, S. (2000) *The Complete Guide to Coaching at Work.* Australia: McGraw Hill

Lightning Source UK Ltd.
Milton Keynes UK
UKOW030831080513

210358UK00001B/1/P